MORPETH TO BELLINGHAM

AND THE ROTHBURY BRANCH

Roger Darsley & Dennis Lovett

Series Editor Vic Mitchell

# Middleton Press

Front cover: The terminus of the branch at Rothbury is the classic view of the station and shed, though it was rarely photographed in colour. In 1953, a 'Gardens' special or perhaps a race day train was in the platform, whilst class J21 0-6-0 no. 65110 was being coaled and watered. The turntable was used to reach the shed, but also to allow the engine to run round its train. (Colour-Rail.com)

Rear cover upper: The 'Wansbeck Wanderer' a joint SLS / RCTS railtour, has reached Bellingham station, hauled by class 4MT 2-6-0 no. 43129 on 29th September 1963. (Colour-Rail.com)

Lower: This view of Bellingham station buildings is from inside the 'Carriages Tea Room' at the station platform on 15th June 2015. The BR Southern Region class 438 TC Mk 1 coaches are part of the Bellingham Heritage Centre. (R.R.Darsley)

Readers of this book may be interested in the following societies:

Bellingham Heritage Centre
Station Yard, Bellingham, NE48 2DG
www.bellingham-heritage.org.uk

North British Railway Study Group
www.nbrstudygroup.co.uk

Railway Correspondence & Travel Society, North East Branch
c/o M. Snowball, 3, Dymock Court, Tudor Grange, Kenton, Newcastle-upon-Tyne NE3 2FH
www.rcts.org.uk

Published March 2016

ISBN 978 1 908174 87 1

© *Middleton Press, 2016*

Design Deborah Esher

Published by
    Middleton Press
    Easebourne Lane
    Midhurst
    West Sussex
    GU29 9AZ
Tel: 01730 813169
Email: info@middletonpress.co.uk
www.middletonpress.co.uk

Printed in the United Kingdom by Henry Ling Limited, at the Dorset Press, Dorchester, DT1 1HD

INDEX

15	Angerton	59	Fontburn Halt	118	Reedsmouth shed
119	Bellingham (North Tyne)	49	Fontburn Reservoir	67	Rothbury
86	Blaxter Quarry	63	Forestburngate	77	Rothbury shed
64	Brinkburn	81	Knowesgate	23	Scotsgap
108	Broomhope	37	Longwitton	33	Scotsgap Junction
99	Catcleugh Reservoir	11	Meldon	111	Steel
43	Ewesley	19	Middleton North	87	Summit Cottages
62	Ewesley Quarry	1	Morpeth	89	Woodburn
47	Fontburn Viaduct	115	Reedsmouth		

ACKNOWLEDGEMENTS

We are grateful for the assistance received from many of those mentioned in the photographic credits and also to The late H. D. Bowtell, S. Fee, J. E. Hay, A. Hayward, W. Hinds, E. Maxwell, A. P. McLean, G. W. N. Sewell and J. W. Yellowlees (ScotRail). Our thanks also to staff of Bellingham Heritage Centre, Woodburn, the Northumberland Record Office, Tyne & Wear Museum Archives and Northumbrian Water Ltd.

1. As built, Morpeth to Reedsmouth was the main operating route but when the Scotsgap to Rothbury branch was completed, Morpeth to Rothbury became the main line. (A.E.Young)

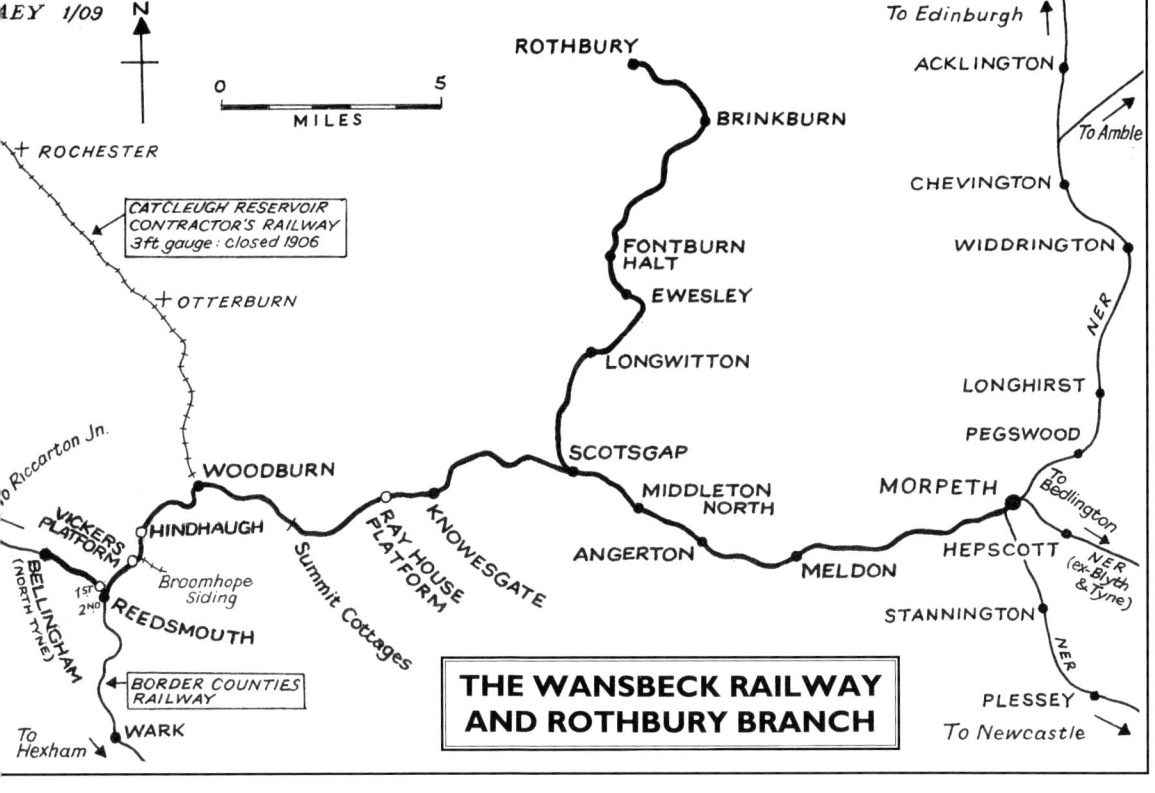

GEOGRAPHCAL SETTING

The line between Morpeth and Bellingham follows the rich agricultural valley of the River Wansbeck (nicknamed the Wanney) which rises above Sweethope Lough on the Ray Estate on the edge of the Forelaws Forest and flows through Morpeth before entering the North Sea near Newbiggin-on-Sea.

Beyond Knowesgate, the line climbs to the south side of Ray Fell, where it reaches 850ft above sea level. To the south is the Great Wanney Crag and Little Wanney Crag, which are referred to locally as 'the Wanneys'.

South-west of Woodburn, in the area known as Ridsdale, there were rich mineral deposits of both iron and coal. The coal was burnt to produce coke, which is used in the iron-making process. The high quality pig iron was in great demand and these facilities were linked by waggonway. This was one of the reasons for promoting the railway, as the iron producers found it difficult to transport the output to Newcastle, where it was used by the engineering companies. The Ridsdale facilities were acquired by the Elswick Iron Company in 1864, following which the iron ore was transported and the blast furnaces closed down. W.G. Armstrong formed his engineering company in Elswick, Newcastle in 1847 and later took over the Ridsdale facilities. A branch line at Broomhope was built to serve the workings which in 1876 had new kilns built at the end of it. By 1879 cheaper imports resulted in the closure of the Ridsdale works, but the site at Broomhope was used by Armstrong (and later Vickers Armstrong) for the testing of naval guns, manufactured by the company at Elswick. A small halt known as Vickers Platform was provided for staff travelling to and from the test site.

Beyond Woodburn, the line followed the valley of the River Rede, which flows into the North Tyne at Redesmouth (please note the railway name of the junction station was Reedsmouth). Here the line joined the Border Counties Line from Hexham via a south-facing junction.

The final two miles to Bellingham over the Border Counties line followed the valley of the River North Tyne, this route providing the only access to Bellingham after closure of the Border Counties line to all traffic in 1958. By 1963 Bellingham, too, was isolated from the rail network.

The Rothbury branch from Scotsgap climbed towards Longwitton station where shortly after leaving the station the line reached a height of 694ft above sea level. Near Fontburn the line crossed the River Font on a 12 arch stone viaduct, which still stands to this day. Here a large reservoir was constructed between 1902 and 1908. Beyond Fontburn, the line reached 650ft above sea level. For the final descent to the terminus at Rothbury, the line followed the valley of the River Coquet, which gives its name to the area around Rothbury of Coquetdale.

All the Ordnance Survey maps are to the scale of 25ins to 1 mile, with north at the top unless indicated otherwise. They are from the 1893 edition.

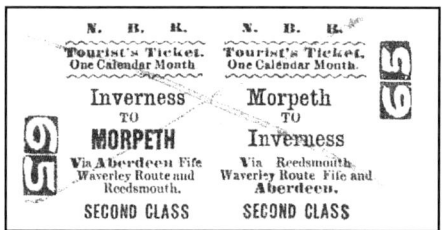 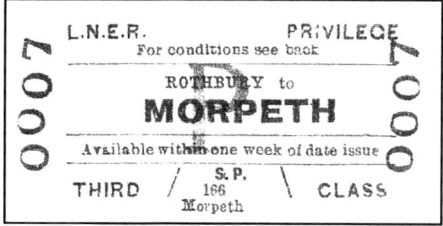

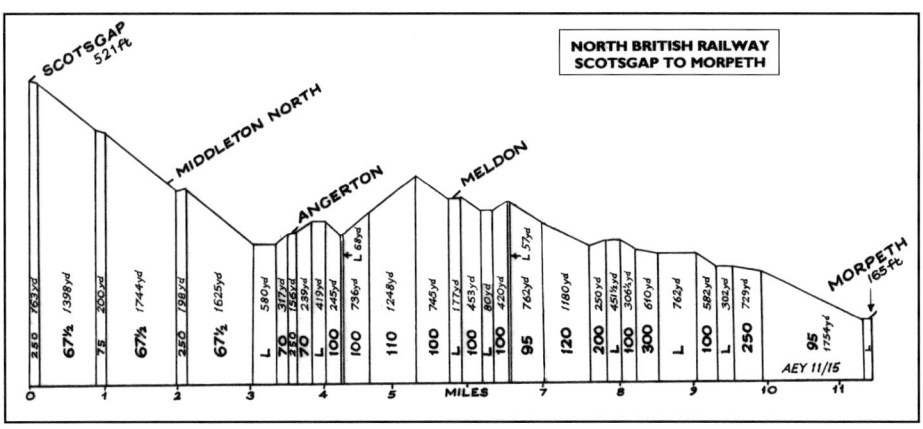
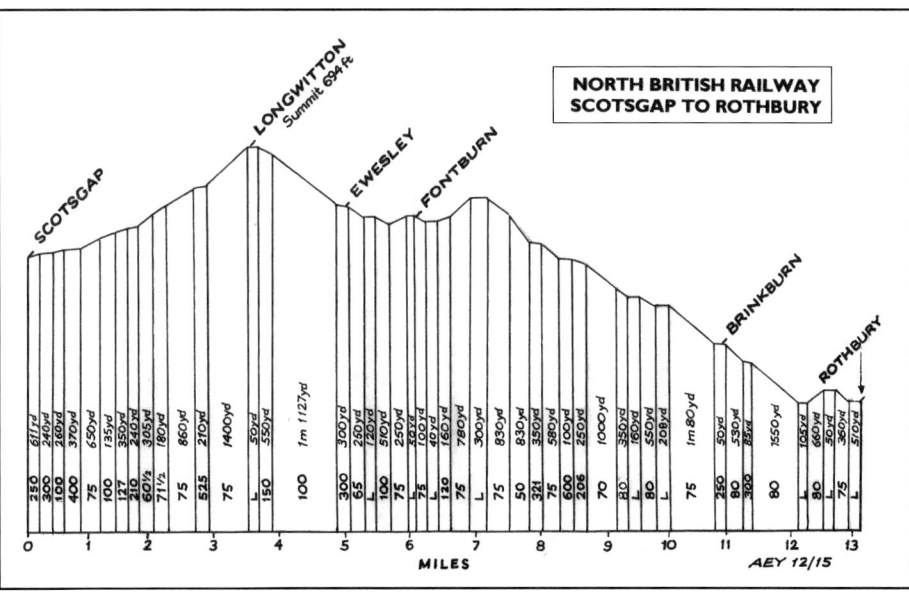
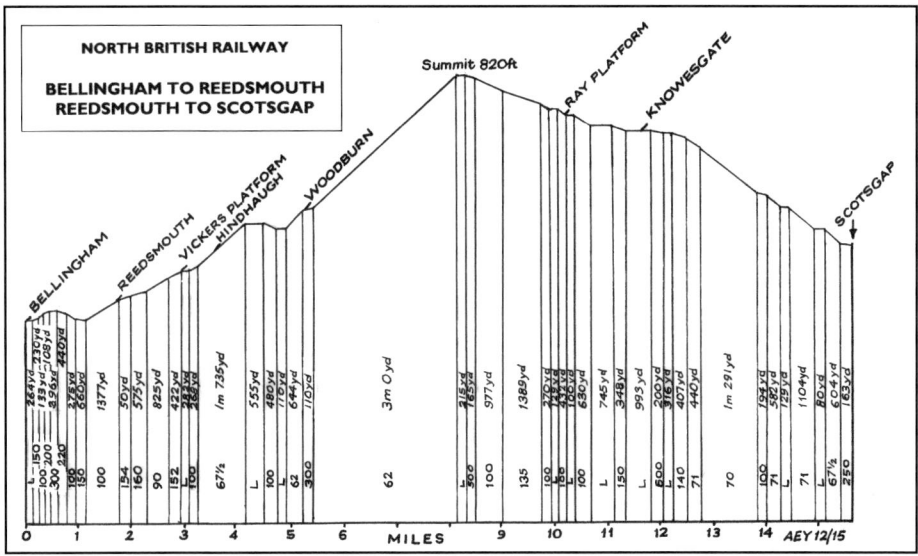

Gradient Profiles (A.E. Young)

HISTORICAL BACKGROUND

Morpeth to Reedsmouth - The Wanney Line

The Wansbeck Railway Act was authorised in 1859 to build a line from Morpeth to Reedsmouth where it would form a junction with the Border Counties Railway, which had opened through Reedsmouth on 2nd September 1861.

The Wansbeck Railway opened from Morpeth to Scotsgap on 23rd July 1862 and initially the company used the Blyth & Tyne Railway station in Morpeth as its eastern terminus. This was adjacent to, but independent from, the North Eastern Railway station, which had opened on 1st March 1847. To reach the Blyth & Tyne station the Wansbeck Railway crossed the East Coast Main Line on a bridge and then reversed on to the Blyth & Tyne. The Blyth & Tyne Railway had obtained its Act to build a branch into Morpeth from Bedlington on 4th August 1853. It opened to goods traffic in October 1857 and to passengers on 1st April 1858.

Our line was extended from Scotsgap to Knowesgate in October 1863 and throughout to Reedsmouth, where a junction was formed with the Border Counties Railway, on 1st May 1865.

The Wansbeck Railway became part of North British Railway on 21st July 1872 and the Blyth & Tyne part of the North Eastern Railway in the same year. The North British Railway had its own aspirations to take over the Blyth & Tyne, as it would have given them an independent route into industrial Newcastle. Just as they had blocked the Border Counties line from reaching Newcastle, the NER once again thwarted the NBR in its efforts to reach Newcastle-upon-Tyne, where it had planned to open its own terminus. The NBR finally gained running rights into Newcastle from Hexham, although it paid the heavy price of having to reciprocate by allowing the NER to haul express trains between Berwick and Edinburgh in return.

The NBR and the NER reached agreement on 8th August 1872 to build a link from the Wansbeck line into the North Eastern station, thus enabling the bridge over the East Coast Main Line into the Blyth & Tyne terminus to be abandoned. Morpeth station was enlarged between 1874 and 1880 enabling the Blyth & Tyne trains to also use the main line station. Their old terminus was then relegated to goods use.

The opening of a major Army training camp at Otterburn in 1911 brought a large increase in traffic to the line both in the form of troop trains and also in the movement of goods and equipment. A number of target railways for armament practice were built on the site allowing targets to be moved across the site on rails.

At the Grouping on 1st January 1923, the line became part of the London & North Eastern Railway. Not surprisingly, the outbreak of World War II on 3rd September 1939 saw considerable increases of troop trains and goods trains carrying armoured vehicles and equipment to and from Otterburn camp, principally through Woodburn which served as its main railhead. This traffic continued to flourish until the end of National Service in 1963.

Upon nationalisation on 1st January 1948, the newly-formed British Railways North Eastern Region incorporated former LNER Scottish Area lines in England, with the Morpeth – Reedsmouth and the Rothbury branch transferring to the North Eastern Region of British Railways.

Passenger services on the Wansbeck line ceased on 15th September 1952. Goods trains continued, with Bellingham continuing to receive a weekly goods train after the closure of the Border Counties line to freight traffic on 1st September 1958. It closed on 11th November 1963, when the line west of Woodburn closed. Services continued between Morpeth and Woodburn, to serve the Ministry of Defence facilities at Otterburn until 29th September 1966.

The goods yards between Morpeth and Middleton North, and Longwitton and Rothbury, all closed on 11th November 1963; those between Scotsgap and Woodburn followed on 3rd October 1966. The line was closed completely between Scotsgap and Rothbury, as well as Woodburn and Reedsmouth, on 11th November 1963, and between Morpeth and Woodburn on 3rd October 1966.

The last passenger train to run was on 2nd October 1966. It was a special between Morpeth and Woodburn organised by The Gosforth Round Table. It operated from Newcastle to Woodburn and back as "The Wansbeck Piper". The line closed throughout on the following day.

A second Army camp opened at Redesdale in 1972, but it was too late to save the Wanney. The camp closed in 2003 and the site is now incorporated into the Otterburn facility.

Scotsgap to Rothbury - The Rothbury Branch

The Northumberland Central Railway was incorporated on 28th July 1863 to build a line from the Wansbeck Railway line near Hartburn to Ford via Rothbury, with a branch to Coldstream (Cornhill) on the Berwick & Kelso Railway. In 1867, plans for the proposed route north of Rothbury were abandoned. The line from Scotsgap to Rothbury did however open on 19th October 1870. On 1st February 1872, the Northumberland Central Railway became part of the NBR.

This delightful sign was on the former station building at Scotsgap on 3rd September 2014. The accurate representation is of a North British Holmes C class J36 0-6-0. (D.A.Lovett)

PASSENGER SERVICES

The justification of the line was to transport minerals to Newcastle via Morpeth, but this was short-lived. The line mainly relied on agriculture to support the sparse passenger services. After the opening of the Rothbury branch, the Reedsmouth line became the branch and Rothbury the more important with trains splitting and joining at Scotsgap.

Just before the Grouping in 1923, the last year of North British Railway ownership, the line saw just three trains a day in each direction. The first train in the morning from Reedsmouth would join the Morpeth train from Rothbury and conveyed through coaches to Newcastle. Likewise, the early evening departure from Newcastle also dropped coaches at Morpeth, which then worked forward to Scotsgap providing early evening arrival times at both Reedsmouth and Rothbury. Additional trains were worked between Reedsmouth and Scotsgap on Tuesdays.

Livestock markets existed at Morpeth, Rothbury and Scotsgap which all generated additional traffic on market days.

1895 timetable showing both the Wansbeck and Rothbury services. This extract is from the Middleton Press Bradshaw Timetable reprint.

July 1948

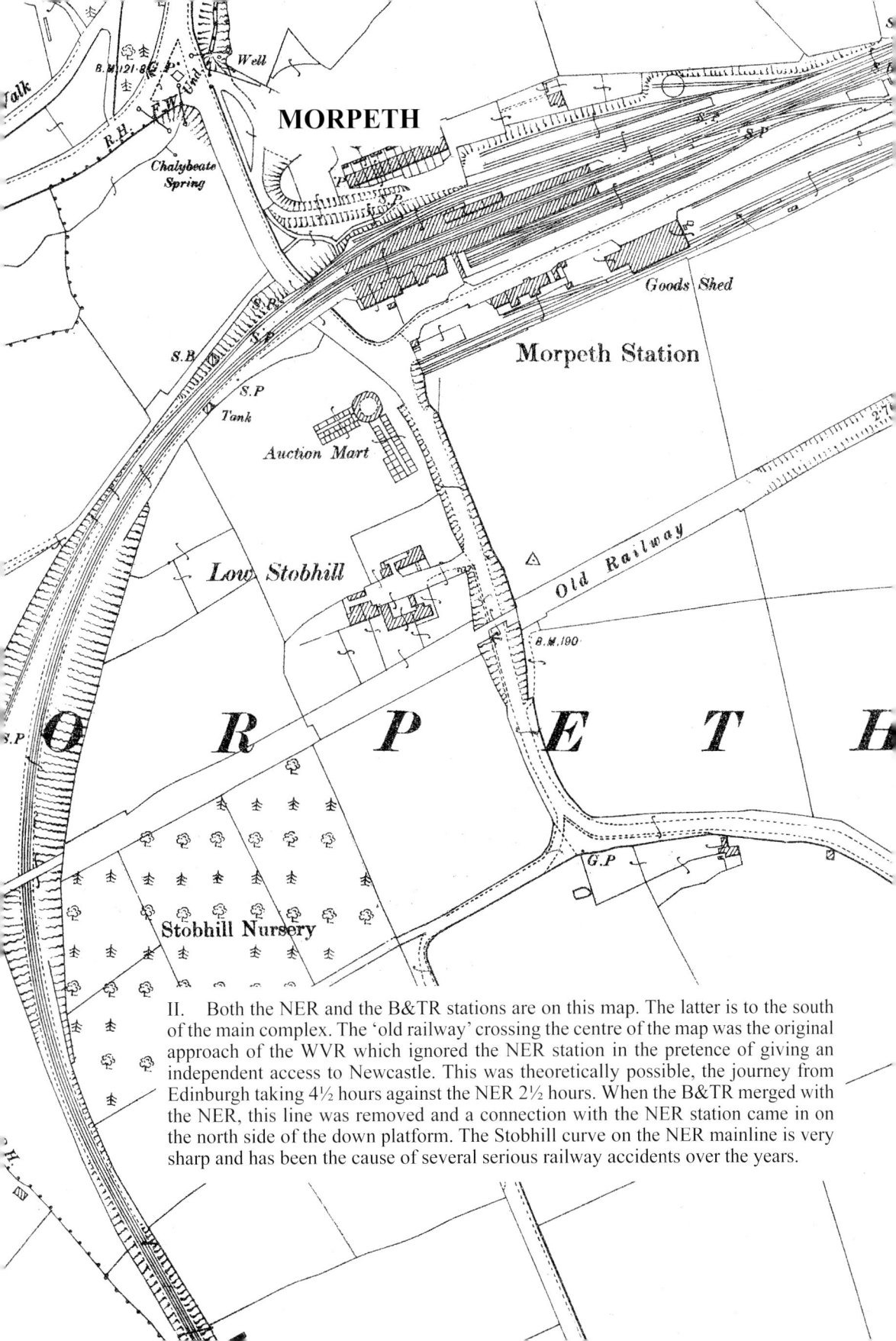

II. Both the NER and the B&TR stations are on this map. The latter is to the south of the main complex. The 'old railway' crossing the centre of the map was the original approach of the WVR which ignored the NER station in the pretence of giving an independent access to Newcastle. This was theoretically possible, the journey from Edinburgh taking 4½ hours against the NER 2½ hours. When the B&TR merged with the NER, this line was removed and a connection with the NER station came in on the north side of the down platform. The Stobhill curve on the NER mainline is very sharp and has been the cause of several serious railway accidents over the years.

1. This aerial view shows the B&TR station on the right-hand side of the station approach road and the NER station on the left. After amalgamation, the B&TR buildings became the goods station for Morpeth, with trains for Ashington and Blyth leaving from the bay platforms. (M.Halbert coll.)

2. Most of the B&TR buildings at Morpeth are still in existence though used for commercial and residential purposes. This is the passenger station building largely unchanged in the 1960s. It opened on 1st April 1858 and closed to Wansbeck trains on 3rd March 1872 and to all passenger traffic on 24th May 1880. (Armstrong Railway Photographic Trust - ARPT)

3. This shows the opening day of the new access line to the NER station. The agreement was authorised on 8th August 1872 and the 1847 station was redesigned between 1874 and 1880. The island platform awnings have not yet been built. The locomotive is an NBR 4-4-0T R class D51 probably no.72 *Morpeth* built in 1880. (R.W.Lynn coll.)

4. This is the Morpeth station in the 1950s. Scotsgap has been spelt in various ways over the years. The NBR tended to have advertisements for 'The Scotsman' slung beneath their station signs. The Station Master is in full regalia. (M.Halbert coll.)

MORPETH.
A telegraph station.
HOTEL.—Queen's Head.

MARKET DAY.—Wednesday.
FAIRS.—Wednesday before Whitsuntide, June, Wednesday before Martinmas.
RACES at Cottingwood in April and September.
BANKERS.—W. H. Lambton and Company.

This borough has a population of 13,794, who return one member, and are employed in the woollen trade. The town was built by Vanburgh. It has a fine suspension bridge, by Telford. The gate of the old castle is worth a visit. Turner, the botanist, Gibbon, the herbalist, and Morrison, the Chinese scholar, born in 1782, were natives; and here Horsley, the learned author of *Britannia Romana*, was a minister. In the vicinity is *Mitford*, seat of Mrs. Mitford.

Extract from Bradshaw's Guide for 1866.
(reprinted by Middleton Press 2011)

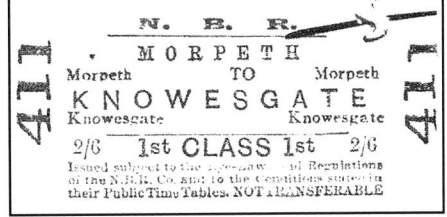

5. The imposing station buildings used to provide a full range of passenger services, but are now available for rent with a ticket office open for limited hours. The NER tiled map has survived and has been joined by a colourful mural done by local school children. Though the photograph, taken on 21st August 2001, is relatively modern, the exterior of the building has not changed greatly over the years. (A.E.Young)

6. This photograph of 5th September 1955 shows the Scotsgap platform with the simplified station board and the full canopies on the island platform. The East Coast main line runs between the main platforms. (H.C.Casserley)

7. G5 (NER O) class 0-4-4T no. 67296 waits at the west end of the island platform to depart with its one coach train for Rothbury. (W.A.Camwell/SLS)

8. The last revenue freight from Rothbury arrived at Morpeth with J21 (NER C) class 0-6-0 no. 65035 as motive power. It has been photographed passing Morpeth South signal box. The signal box was opened in 1891 with 28 levers. In 1936 it was renamed Wansbeck SB and signalled the Reedsmouth branch only. (J.W.Armstrong/ARPT)

9.   One of the popular excursion trains over the normally closed lines was the RCTS/SLS "Wansbeck Wanderer" on 9th November 1963. A sparkling class 4MT 2-6-0 no. 43129 has arrived from Newcastle on the down main line and will have to draw the train forward to run around it, to access the branch line. (V.Wake/ARPT).

10.   Just to show us that Morpeth station is still with us in the 21st Century, we have included class 91 Bo-Bo WE no. 91109 passing through the station on 16th April 2011, with a northbound East Coast train. At the time of writing, the station was served by the Northern, Arriva Cross Country and Virgin Trains East Coast franchises. (R.Sweet)

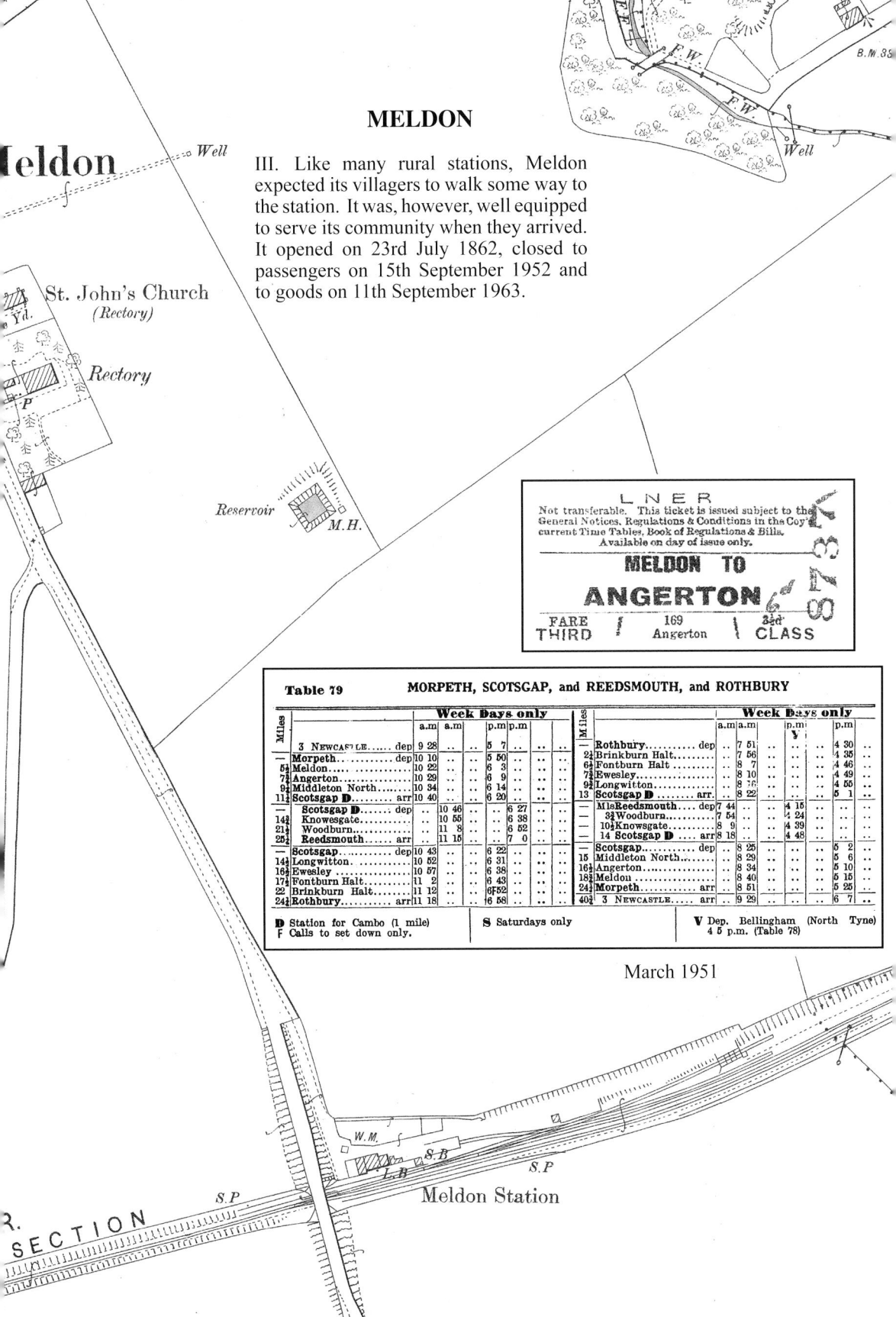

11. This 1904 post card shows the well built station and the road, carried over the track by a substantial bridge. The village is up the hill with the Rectory and St. Johns church just visible in the trees. (J.Alsop coll.)

12. By 1910, the station staff have turned the single platform into a riot of floral beds with ivy and roses climbing the wall. The small signal box is at the east end of the platform. (J.Alsop coll.)

13. The signal box was opened in 1893 with eight levers. It was closed in 1940 and replaced by a ground frame. The refuge siding allowed a train to be recessed for another to pass. (R.W.Lynn coll.)

14. In the last days of the branch, class 4MT 2-6-0 nos. 43063 and 43000 coupled back to back took the 'Wansbeck Piper' rail tour, organised by Gosforth Round Table, on 2nd October 1966 to Woodburn, which by then was the end of the line. The locomotives are entering Meldon, travelling west. The station survives as a private residence. (R.W.Lynn coll.)

ANGERTON

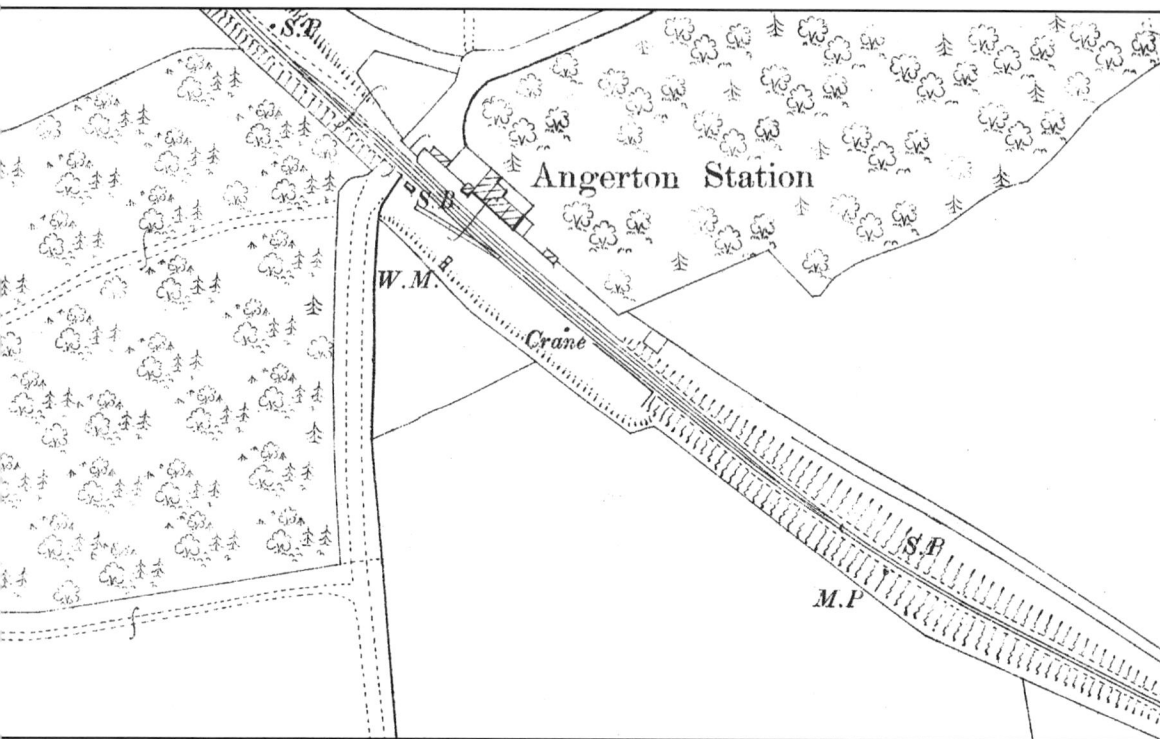

IV. The station was in a rich agricultural area, but housing was dispersed. The expenditure on a road bridge was avoided by providing a gated crossing. It opened on 23rd July 1862, closed to passengers on 15th September 1952 and to goods on 11th November 1963.

Bradshaw's Timetable for April 1910.

15. The attractive buildings are enhanced in 1903 by the gardens and carefully tended climbing plants. A North British four-plank wagon waits in the siding. If the two people are prospective passengers, it is hoped a train arrived before the platform oil lamps needed lighting.
(J.Alsop coll.)

16. This view looks west towards the level crossing and was taken from the goods bank, though the crane is missing. The date was 8th August 1954. The station had a ground frame opened in 1893 and closed in 1964. This was housed in a hut on the platform but was not a block post.
(A.G.Ellis/N.E.Stead coll.)

17. J27 (NER P3) class 0-6-0 no. 65789 was working the demolition train back to Morpeth in 1967. It carried the headboard 'Farewell South Blyth Steam'. After Reedsmouth shed closed, locomotives were supplied from Blyth and the headboard refers to the closure of South Blyth shed. (N.E.Stead)

18. The fine station building became a private residence, seen here on 6th April 1977. (A.E.Young)

MIDDLETON NORTH

V. A simple goods loop and small station building sufficed for Middleton. The station was near to the village it served. The station closed to passengers on 15th September 1952 and to goods on 11th November 1963.

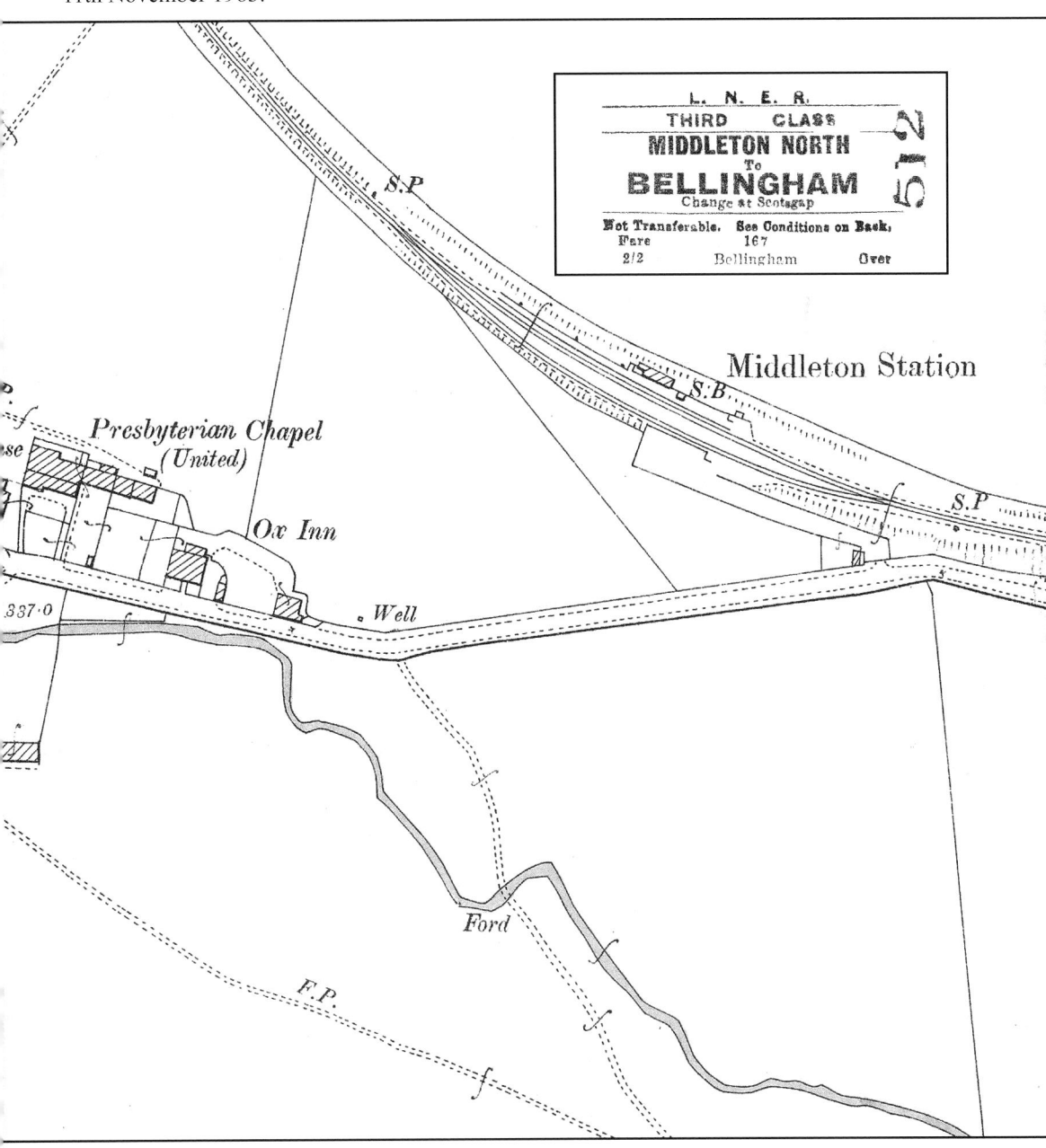

19. Requiring an order of expenditure less than the stations we have seen so far, Middleton was a wood-boarded, single-storeyed building. It looks as though all that was required was present. What ever happened to Epps's Cocoa? (R.W.Lynn coll.)

20. Still in North British days, the train to Rothbury arrives with a flourish. It is hauled by a D51 class 4-4-0T and included a through coach from Newcastle. (M.Halbert coll.)

21. The station was named Middleton (North) on 1st July 1923 when the newly formed LNER found it had several Middleton stations. The station buildings had been repainted. A J35 (Reid B) class 0-6-0 is in the station with a directors inspection saloon. (R.W.Lynn coll.)

22. The passenger service has ceased and there appears to be no freight. The station had a short-lived signal box between 1893 and 1900 along with a crossing loop during this period. The Goods Loop was left. In 2015 only part of the derelict platform remained. (C.J.B.Sanderson/ARPT.)

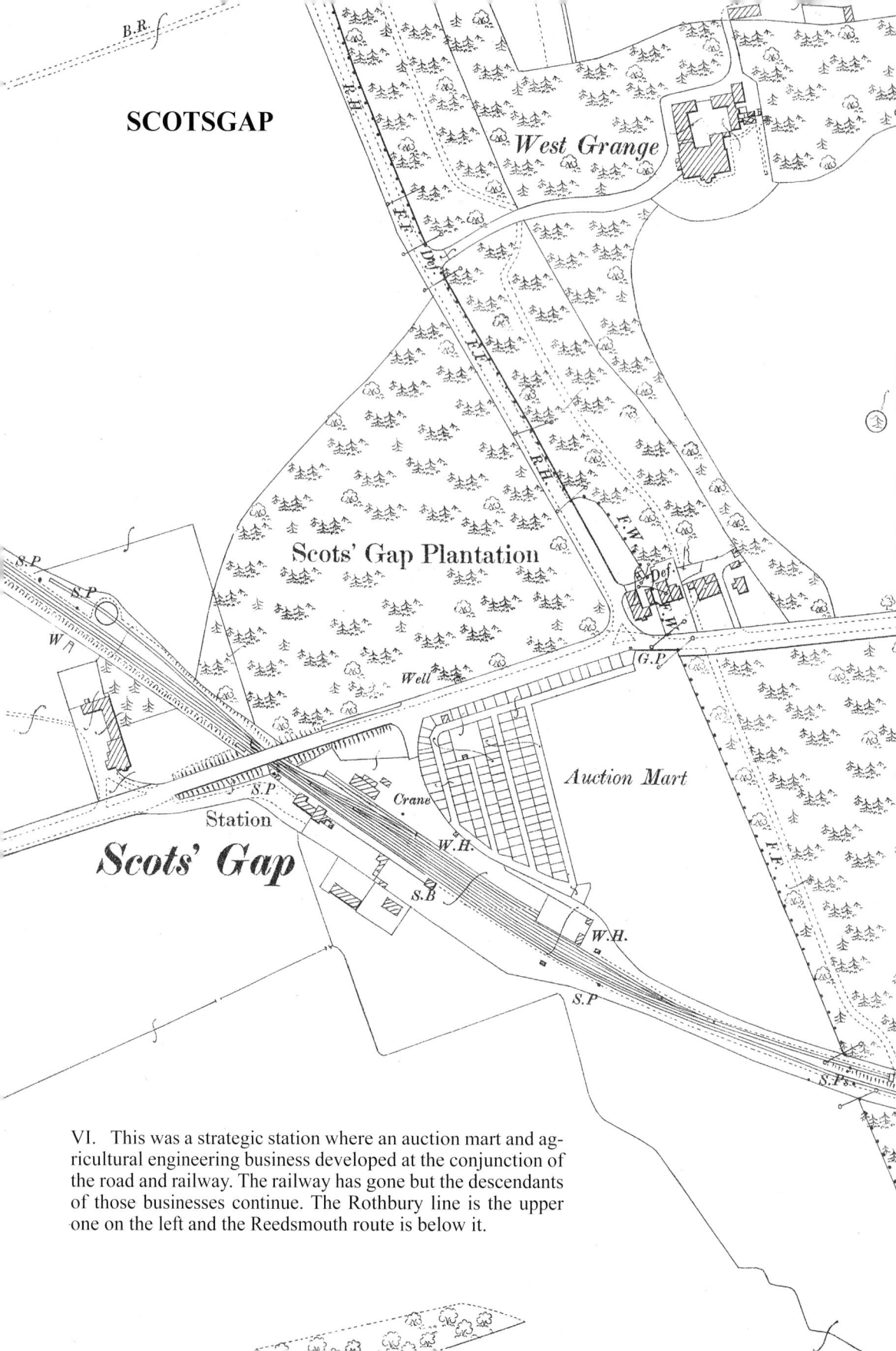

VI. This was a strategic station where an auction mart and agricultural engineering business developed at the conjunction of the road and railway. The railway has gone but the descendants of those businesses continue. The Rothbury line is the upper one on the left and the Reedsmouth route is below it.

23. The station and its staff are viewed in NBR days with D51 class 4-4-0T no. 72 which, along with no. 73, was a regular on the branch. (R.W.Lynn coll.)

24. Looking to the west, this scene shows the station in about 1904. The original signal box is on the platform. It opened in 1893 with 30 levers, but was later moved to the east end and located at ground level. It controlled a crossing loop and closed with the line in 1966. Following the move, a lamp hut or storage shed was erected near the bridge and remained there in 2015. (J.Alsop coll.)

25. Class J36 0-6-0 LNER no. 5343 pauses at Scotsgap in 1946 after arrival from Morpeth ready to continue its journey westwards. Trains were often joined or split here between the two routes serving Reedsmouth or Rothbury. (R.W.Lynn coll.)

26. A Morpeth bound train waits in the station for the signal. G5 class 0-4-4T no. 67925 is in an early British Railways livery. Scotsgap has been spelt as two words with or without an apostrophe but in the last timetable form it was Scotsgap (for Cambo). Cambo was the estate village for Wallington Hall. (N.E.Stead)

27. The passenger trains all carried wreaths on the last day of passenger service, which was 13th September 1952. Here is class J21 (NER C) 0-6-0 no. 65042 passing a train already at the single platform. (J.W.Armstrong/ARPT)

28. The freight service continued on the Wansbeck Valley line and here class J25 (NER P1) 0-6-0 no. 65727, complete with small snow plough, works a goods train into the station. This locomotive was a North Blyth engine and was withdrawn from that shed on 31st October 1961. (N.E.Stead)

29. Class J27 0-6-0 no. 65860 trundles past the signal box with a freight from Morpeth. Two early versions of container wagons are in the train's make-up. The date is 13th April 1965 and the freight service ended on 3rd October 1966. (N.E.Stead)

30. Scotsgap had a permanent way inspection trolley kept in a shed at right angles to the operating track. These little vehicles were often seen in their sheds, but not so often being manoeuvred onto the track. (R.W.Lynn coll.)

31. West of the road bridge was the coaling stage and watering site. 4MT class 2-6-0 no. 43053 is receiving attention before proceeding with its freight train to Woodburn. The points ahead of the locomotive are the actual junction between the lines to Rothbury and Reedsmouth. (M.Burns/ARPT)

32. A class J27 0-6-0 with a military freight is leaving Scotsgap for Woodburn while an industrial locomotive is involved in materials recovery from the Rothbury branch. The 0-4-0DM is probably James J. Fowler no. 23011 of 1945. It was new to the Air Ministry and was the property of W.Bush of Alfreton by March 1962. It was scrapped about April 1983. (R.W.Lynn coll.)

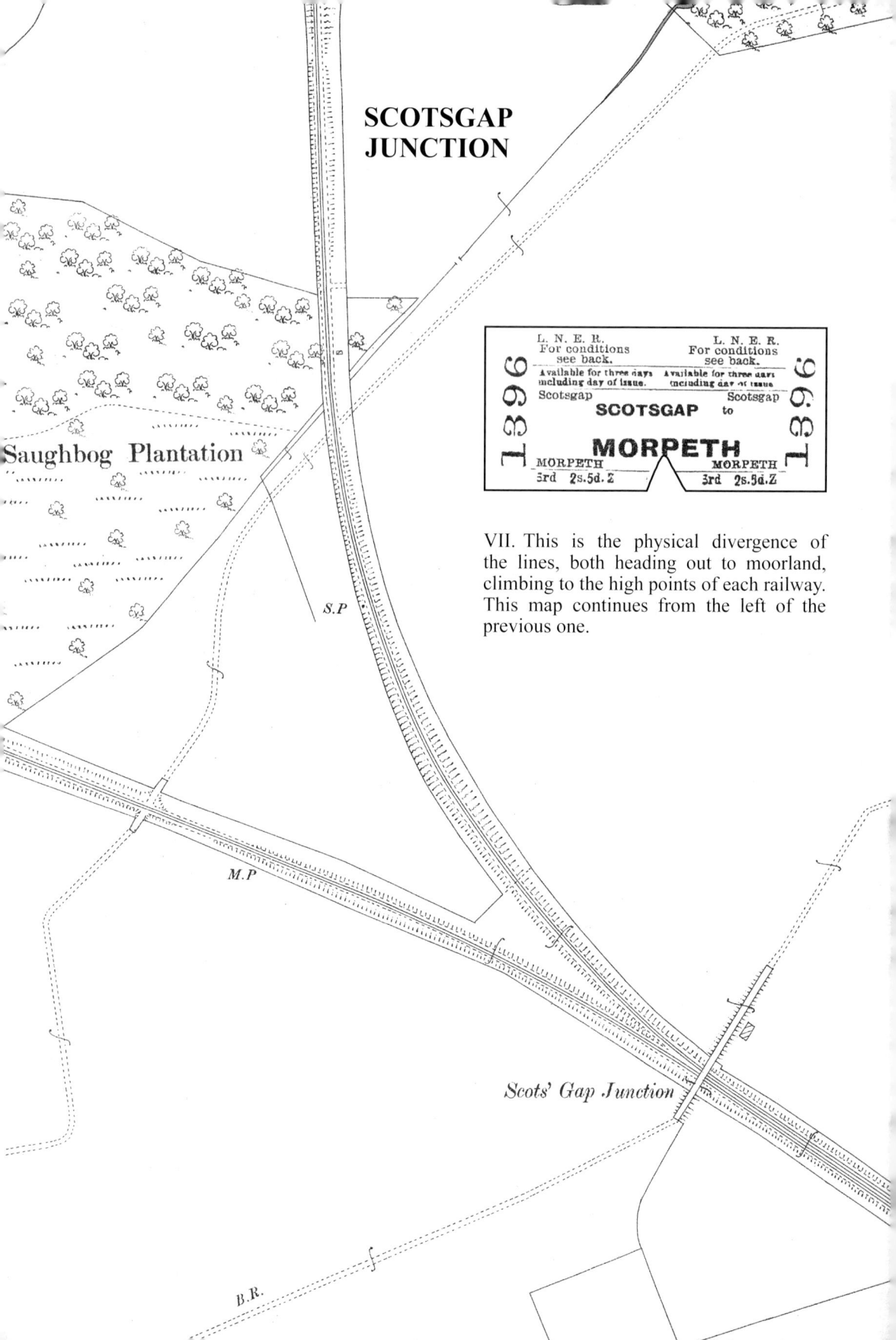

33. This is an iconic photograph of G5 class 0-4-4T LNER no. 1745 leaving Scotsgap with a Rothbury train. While the railway looks like double track, it is two single lines, the nearer to Reedsmouth and the farther to Rothbury. (E.E.Smith/ARPT)

34. As we look to the west, J21 class 0-6-0 no. 65119 was arriving from Reedsmouth and crossing the actual junction at Scotsgap. The turntable is on the right. (R.W.Lynn coll.)

35. Bridge 47, a typical NBR farmer's accommodation bridge, is the point of divergence of the two lines. The line to Rothbury is on the left and to Reedsmouth on the right. The bridge at the station is in the distance. (R.W.Lynn coll.)

36. This shows the stub end of the Rothbury branch as seen from a DMU excursion to Bellingham. We shall take advantage of hindsight and follow the line through Longwitton, Ewesley, Fontburn and Brinkburn to Rothbury. (ARPT)

Scotsgap - Rothbury tablet. (R.W.Lynn coll.)

The Rothbury Branch
LONGWITTON

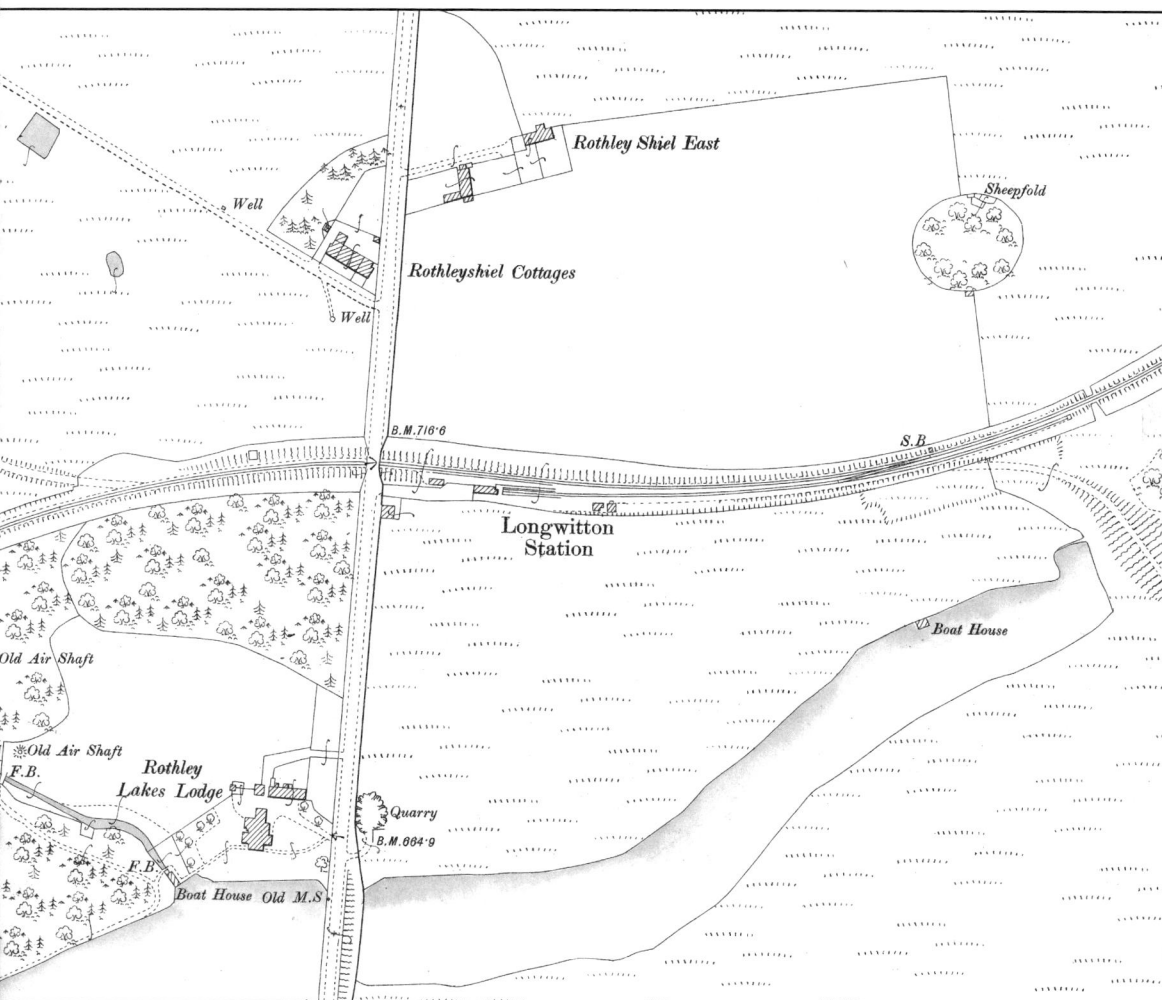

VIII. The station was opened with the branch on 4th November 1870, but was as a private halt named Rothley for the use of the Trevelyan Estate. When the NBR took over the NCR, it was opened to the public and in April 1875 renamed Longwitton. On the left of the map is the track bed of the two mile-long standard gauge line to Greenleighton Quarry operating in the 1880s. A later tramway connected the quarry with the lime kilns, but not with the Rothbury branch. One the right is the track bed of the Longwitton colliery branch. Both sidings had their own industrial locomotives in the early days. The colliery closed by 1890 but the quarry continued until 1968 with road transport.

37.   No photograph has been found of the station as Rothley. The view from the road bridge shows the basic building plus a few sheds and a grounded NBR coach as a store. (N.E.Stead)

38.   A similar view, some years later, shows a van in the short siding and an air of decay. The station has a visible name-board under the eaves of the main building. There was a signal box before 1893, but this was replaced with a NBR hut that closed about 1910. (R.W.Lynn coll.)

39. It is 1952 and a J25 0-6-0 is storming through the station with a special for Rothbury Races. Regular passenger trains ceased on 15th September 1952 and goods traffic followed on 11th November 1963. (J.W.Armstrong/ARPT)

40. In 1956, class J25 0-6-0 no. 65727 trundles more sedately through the station with a freight train for Rothbury. The locomotive is fitted with a small snow plough and up on the bank is a substantial snow fence. As we shall see later, the weather can be very severe. (Colour-Rail.com)

41. Ivatt class 2MT no. 46474 makes an interesting comparison with the more normal NER locomotives. Quite distinct in the Longwitton photographs are the concrete sleepers on this short piece of track. A very short freight was heading to Rothbury. (W.S.Sellar)

42. The wooden platform face and the road bridge remain, with self-seeded trees giving a sylvan air on 3rd September 2014. The sound of trains has been replaced by the sound of horses being exercised along the track bed. (D.A.Lovett)

GREENLEIGHTON QUARRY, LONGWITTON

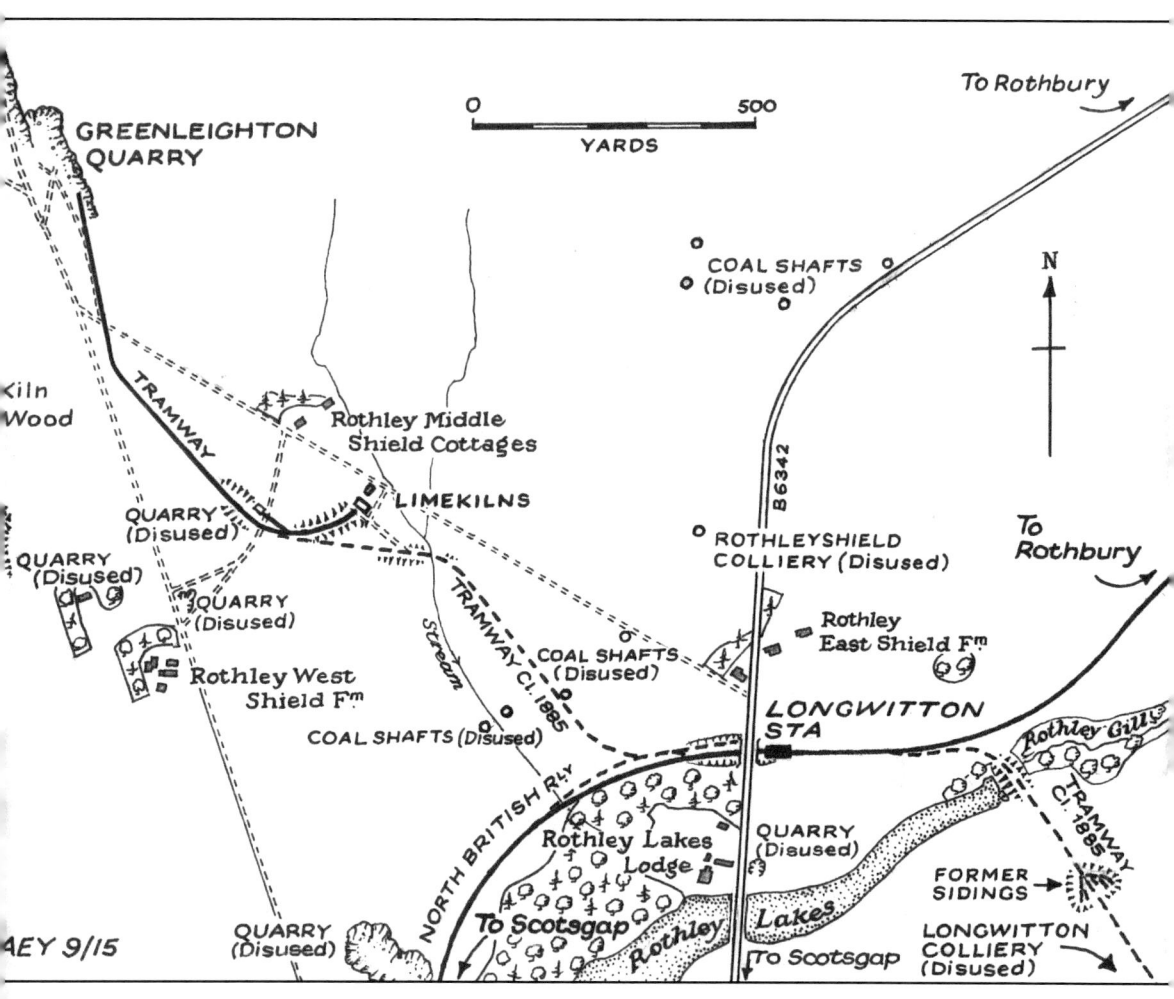

IX. Longwitton Colliery was operated between 1873 and 1885. It had a locomotive *Longwitton* 0-4-0ST Black Hawthorn no. 325 of 1875. It is believed that the original tramway from Longwitton to Greenleighton Lime Kilns and Quarry was narrow gauge when it was worked by the Longwitton Coal & Lime Co. The quarry and lime kilns were reopened by W.T. Bathgate (Limeworks Ltd) and their 2ft gauge line ran from the quarry to the lime kilns only. From 1939 until 1968, when their operation ceased, they had six Ruston Hornsby 4wDM locomotives. They had a smaller quarry at Forestburngate known as Ward's Hill Quarry and two locomotives from Greenleighton spent time there until 1962.

EWESLEY

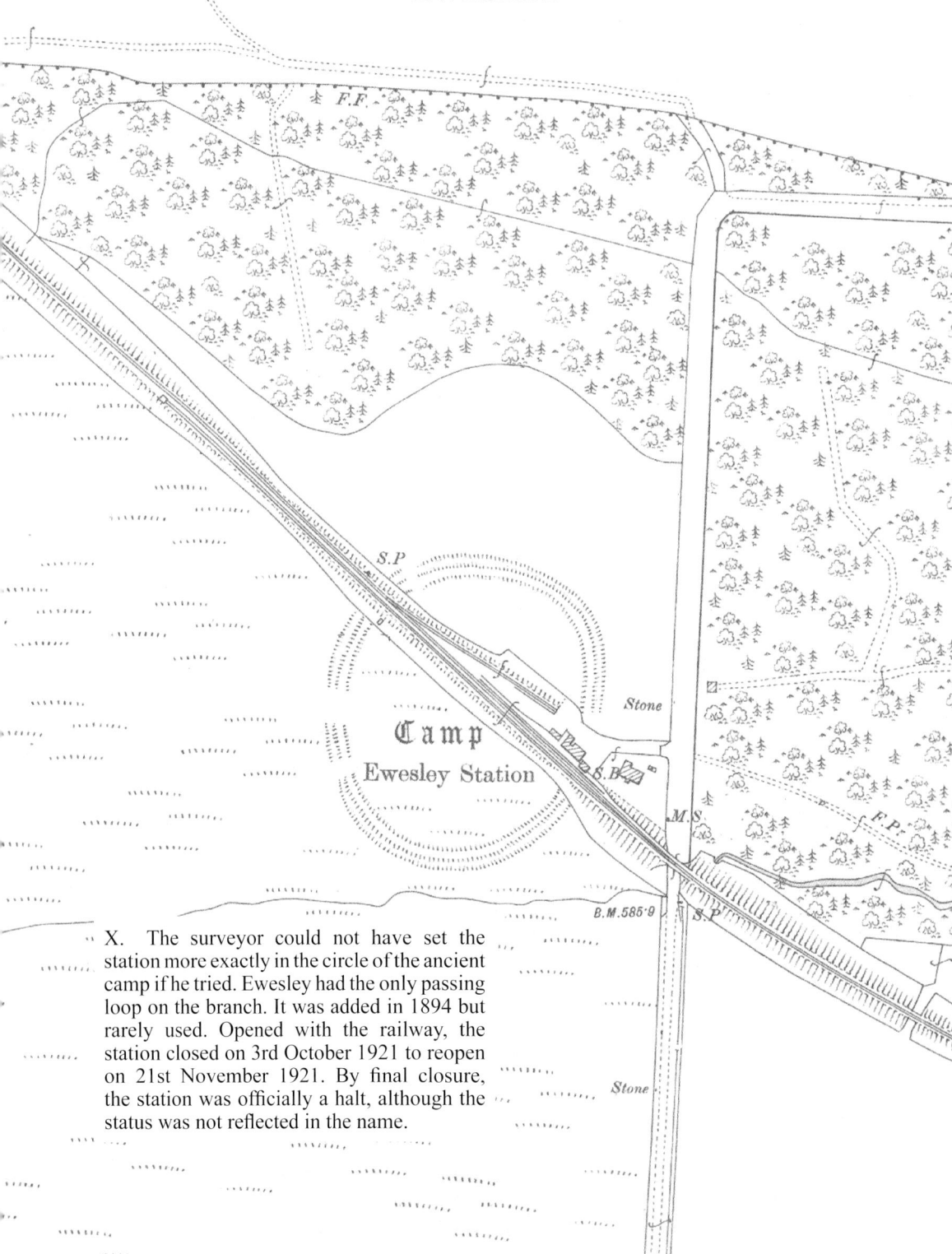

X. The surveyor could not have set the station more exactly in the circle of the ancient camp if he tried. Ewesley had the only passing loop on the branch. It was added in 1894 but rarely used. Opened with the railway, the station closed on 3rd October 1921 to reopen on 21st November 1921. By final closure, the station was officially a halt, although the status was not reflected in the name.

43. From NBR days a quarterly director's special set out to tour the branch lines. Here it is at Ewesley in 1934 and the passing loop is prominent. Besides the directors there was a typist and photographer with the train. (R.W.Lynn coll.)

44. The station master's house was a separate brick building on the north side of the line. The station name was etched out in chippings and plants and faced the line. It was likely to be less visible when the potatoes grew out of the ridges. (R.W.Lynn coll.)

45. This photograph was taken on the 15th July 1952 from one of the ancient camp banks. The 1893 signal box had eight levers, but was closed in 1941. The replacement ground frame lasted as long as the refuge siding that allowed a recessed train to be passed. (A.G.Ellis/R.W.Lynn coll.)

46. A grand view of the moors north of Ewesley can be enjoyed as class J27 0-6-0 no. 65819 approaches the station with a freight from Rothbury. (H.D.Bowtell/R.W.Lynn coll.)

FONTBURN VIADUCT

47. The impressive twelve span viaduct carried the railway 60ft above the River Font. The train would appear to be a Rothbury Races special returning towards Scotsgap with a class J21 or class J25 0-6-0 as locomotive. (Mrs D. Eggleton)

48. In 1870, when the line opened, the viaduct was the major construction in the area, but when the Tynemouth Water Company decided to dam the Font and build a reservoir the scale of building altered. This is the viaduct and the filter beds of the Fontburn Reservoir, seen from the dam wall on 3rd September 2014. (D.A.Lovett)

FONTBURN RESERVOIR

The Newcastle & Gateshead Water Company did not supply Tynemouth and North Shields (now the Metropolitan area of North Tyneside). Tynemouth Corporation took Parliamentary powers to take over the unsatisfactory North Shields Water Company in 1898 and in 1900 the Corporation's Water Committee hired a special train, probably to Ewesley station, to view the prospect of damming the Font Burn.

The committee cut the first sod in October 1901. A hutted camp was provided for workers with a 'main street', a licensed canteen, a navvy mission and a police constable. A school opened in 1905 and remained a school until 1929. It then became a village hall until the 1950s. There was also a shop and post office and at its busiest, the village population reached 450; 250 being employed men.

With the NBR Rothbury branch being so close to the site, extra sidings were put in at Fontburn. A 3ft gauge line served the dam site from interchange sidings with the standard gauge sidings behind Fontburn Halt. In a way that both railways served the cement store. The narrow gauge railway was therefore confined to the site. Besides the steam locomotives, at least 16 horses were used.

The main rundown of activity was 1907-08 and filling the dam commenced on 4th March 1908. On 16th October 1908, the lake was full and in December 1908 the surplus plant was sold off.

Locomotives at Fontburn:

Tattoo	0-4-2ST	Kerr Stuart no. 852 of 1904
Tynemouth	0-4-0ST	Hunslet no. 759 of 1901
Fontburn	0-4-0ST	Hudswell Clarke no. 418 of 1894 (from Catcleugh Otterburn)
Rede	0-4-0ST	W.G.Bagnall no. 1413 of 1894 (from Catcleugh)

49. A hutted camp was built at the northern edge of the Font Burn valley. These were basically wooden buildings, single or in short terraces. The labourer's family lived in a hut but the wife often sub-let one room to single labourers who worked a shift pattern in both work and bed.
(Northumbrian Water Ltd.)

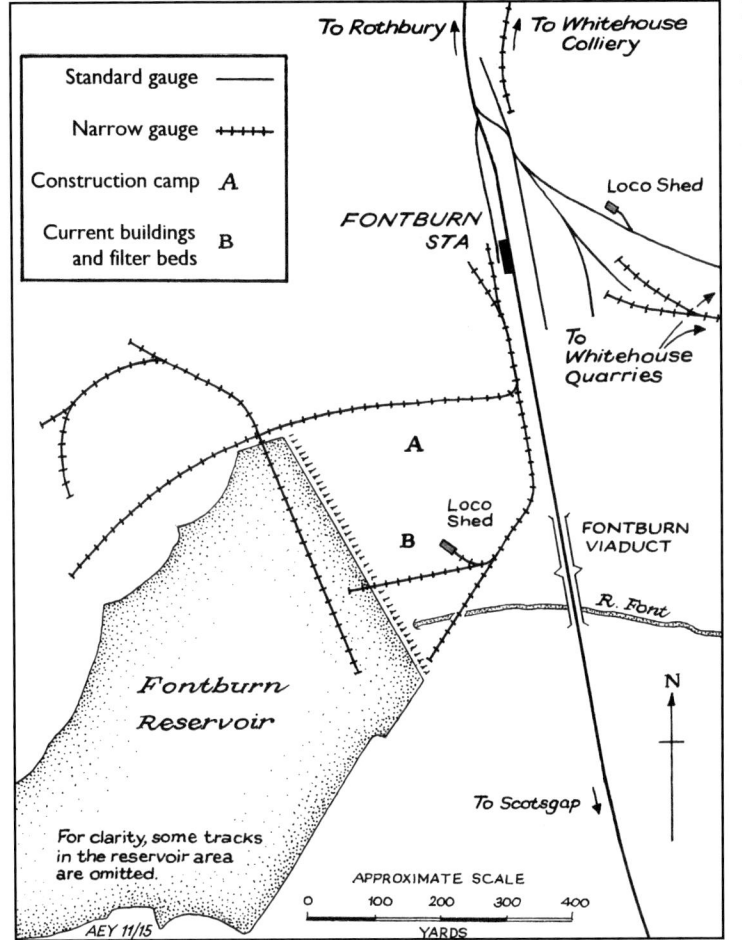

XI. A simplified plan shows the relationship between the Rothbury branch, the narrow gauge line used for constructing the reservoir and those serving local industry. (A.E.Young)

50. This view is from the south across the valley. In the foreground are the first permanent structures. In the middle ground is the 3ft gauge line engine shed, with four rail wagons in front of it. In the background are the main streets of the camp. (Northumbrian Water Ltd.)

51. The first 3ft gauge locomotive on the Fontburn site was *Tattoo* 0-4-2ST Kerr Stuart no. 852 of 1904. This was delivered new in 1904 to Tynemouth Corporation and was a new design for Kerr Stuart who used the name as a class name thereafter. (Northumbrian Water Ltd.)

52. On the left, *Tattoo* is arriving with a train about to pass the workshops and stables on its way to the cement shed. On the right is the standard gauge Rothbury branch with Fontburn Halt just visible in the distance. (Northumbrian Water Ltd.)

53. *Tynemouth* was a 0-4-0ST built by Hunslet, as no. 759 of 1901. It was new to Douglas Corporation on the Isle of Man, as their *Ardwhallin*. Renamed, it was shipped to Fontburn on 20th May 1905. Apparently it still had a brass decoration of the three legs of Man on the chimney. It was sold on to John Best. (ARPT)

54. The third locomotive on the site was *Fontburn* 0-4-0ST Hudswell Clarke no. 418 of 1894 which came from the Newcastle & Gateshead Water Company at Catcleugh, where it was named *Otterburn*. About 1909 it was sold to Blaxters Ltd at Knowesgate, where it was called *Ottercops*. The fourth locomotive at Fontburn also came from Catcleugh and was *Rede* 0-4-0ST W.G.Bagnall no. 1413 of 1894. Later this locomotive was at Masham in North Yorkshire.
(Northumbrian Water Ltd.)

55. Preparations begin for the construction of the dam trench. The steam cranes were 3 tons capacity, standard gauge and eventually six were used on this excavation. The 3ft gauge side tipping wagons are labelled T.C. for Tynemouth Corporation. (Northumbrian Water Ltd.)

56. This view to the northwest, over the embankment trench was taken in August 1904. Two of the steam cranes are on the left. On the right are two cement mixers. Above them, 0-4-0ST *Tattoo* is seen with wagons about to charge the concrete plant. (Northumbrian Water Ltd.)

57. The valve tower is well under construction in this photograph. Beyond the rising dam wall, the roof of the permanent reservoir house is just visible. (Northumbrian Water Ltd.)

58. The job is almost complete. Standard gauge steam crane track is being removed. Some of the huts have also gone. The first water was received at Tynemouth in April. The official council inspection was on 8th September 1909. (Northumbrian Water Ltd.)

FONTBURN HALT

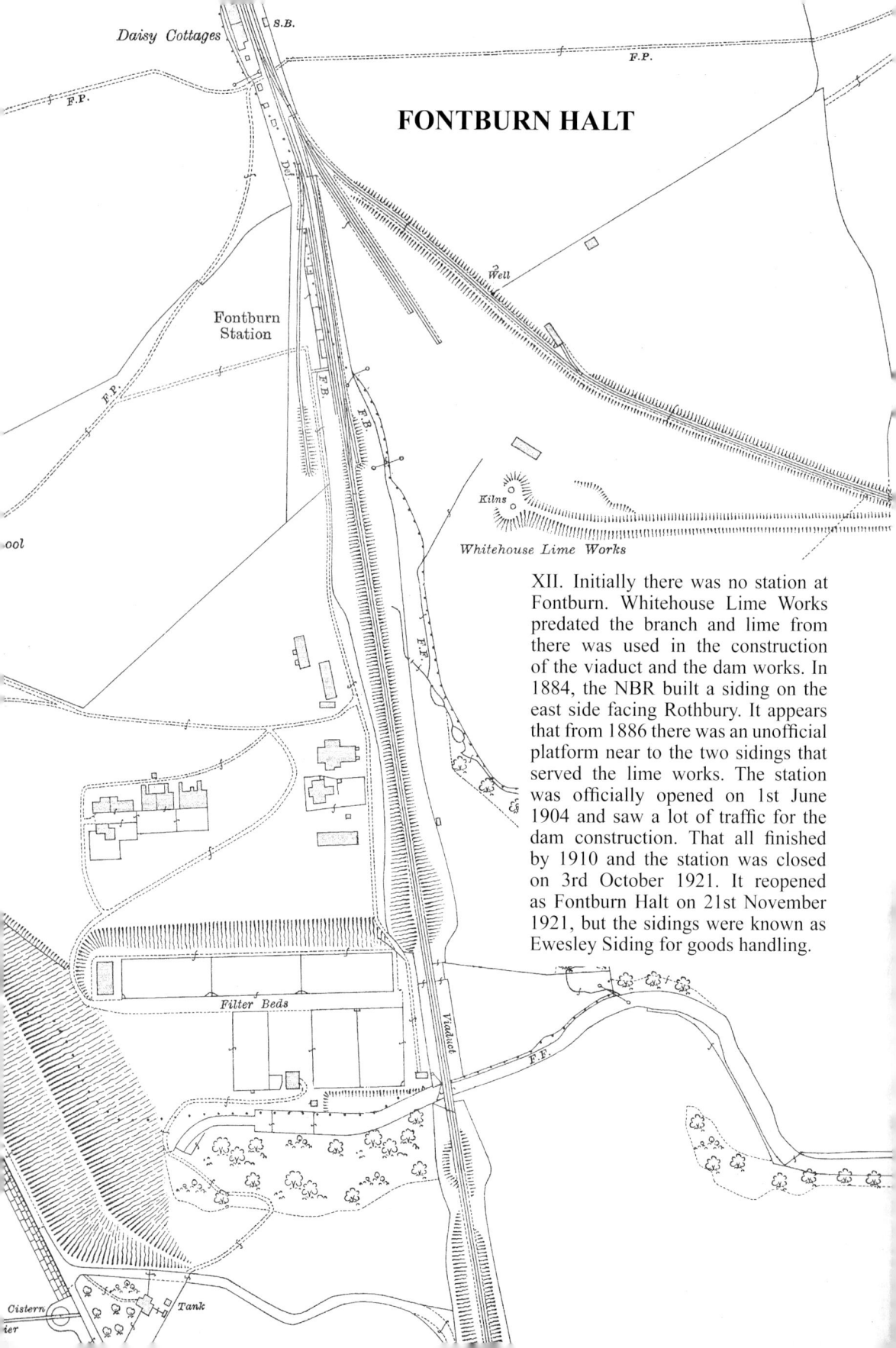

XII. Initially there was no station at Fontburn. Whitehouse Lime Works predated the branch and lime from there was used in the construction of the viaduct and the dam works. In 1884, the NBR built a siding on the east side facing Rothbury. It appears that from 1886 there was an unofficial platform near to the two sidings that served the lime works. The station was officially opened on 1st June 1904 and saw a lot of traffic for the dam construction. That all finished by 1910 and the station was closed on 3rd October 1921. It reopened as Fontburn Halt on 21st November 1921, but the sidings were known as Ewesley Siding for goods handling.

59. This is Fontburn as a station about 1910 with the staff and the crew of NBR no. 33, R class 4-4-0T. Between 1880 and 1883, it carried the name *Bellgrove* and the locomotive was not normally on this branch. The hutted camp would be dismantled and the heyday of construction soon over. (A.E.Young coll.)

60. While the permanent population of the area was small, its remoteness meant that the halt could serve a community purpose. The main building has been replaced by a very small shelter and this survived until closure. (N.E.Stead)

61. Passengers wait to board the train on 13th September 1952. Behind the station was the standard gauge siding to the cement shed and the major interchange point with the dam builder's railway. In 2015 only the concrete fence posts remain to show the site of the halt. (ARPT)

MORPETH BRANCH.—North British.

Miles.	Up.	Week Days only.					Miles.	Down.		Week Days only.			
		mrn	mrn	aft	aft				mrn	aft	aft	aft	aft
—	Reedsmouth...dep.	8 0	1120	4 15	6 5		—	Morpeth ....dep.	9 45	2 15		5 55	
3¾	Woodburn	8 10	1129	4 24	6 14		5¼	Meldon	9 58	2 23		6 8	
10¼	Knowesgate §	8 26	1144	4 39	6 29		7¼	Angerton	10 4	2 34		6 14	
14	Scotsgap¦......arr.	8 35	1153	4 48	6 38		9	Middleton	10 9	2 39		6 19	
—	M ls Rothbury..dep.	8 9	1130	4 29			11	Scotsgap¦.......arr.	1015	2 45		6 25	
—	2¼ Brinkburn	8 14	1135	4 34			—	Scotsgap ......dep.	1017	2 47		6 27	
—	6¾ Fontburn Halt	8 26	1147	4 46			14¾	Longwitton	1026	2 56		6 36	
—	7¾ Ewesley	8 30	1151	4 50			16¾	Ewesley	1031	3 1		6 42	
—	9¾ Longwitton	8 36	1157	4 56			17¾	Fontburn Halt ...	1035	3 5		6 46	
—	13 Scotsgap¦...arr.	8 42	12 3	5 2			21¾	Brinkburn	1045	3 15		6 56	
—	Scotsgap ....dep.	8 44	12 5	5 4			24	Rothbury.....arr.	1051	3 21		7 2	
16	Middleton	8 49	1210	5 9			—	Scotsgap........dep.	1022	2 54 5 8		6H32 6 45	
17¼	Angerton	8 53	1214	5 13			14¾	Knowesgate §	1033	3 5 5 19		6H43 6 56	
19¾	Meldon ...[735, 745]	8 59	1220	5 19			21¾	Woodburn	1047	3 19 5 33		6H57 7 10	
25	Morpeth 734, arr.	9 9	1230	5 29			25	Reedsmouth 809 arr.	1055	3 27 5 41		7H57 7 18	

H Except Tuesdays.   ‡ Station for Cambo (1 mile).   § Station for Kirkwhelpington (1 mile).

Bradshaw's Timetable for June 1922.

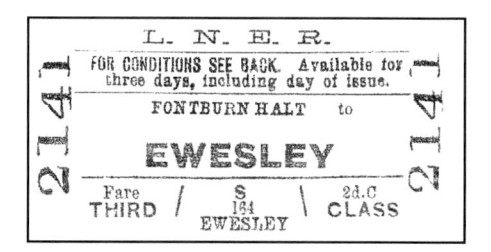

L. N. E. R.
FOR CONDITIONS SEE BACK. Available for three days, including day of issue.
FONTBURN HALT to
EWESLEY
Fare / S 2d.C
THIRD   164   CLASS
     EWESLEY

2144

WHITEHOUSE COLLIERY & RAILWAY COTTAGES

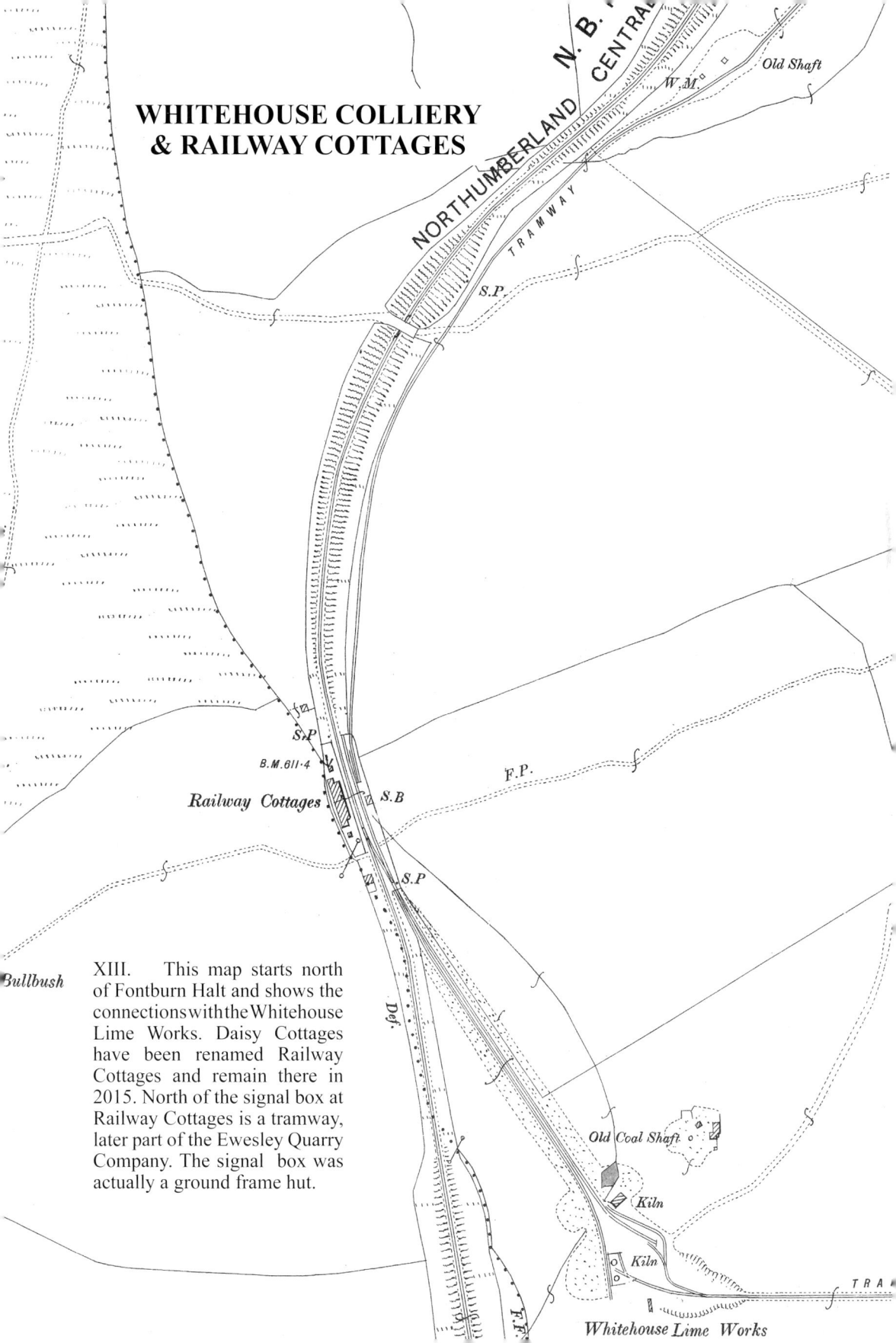

XIII. This map starts north of Fontburn Halt and shows the connections with the Whitehouse Lime Works. Daisy Cottages have been renamed Railway Cottages and remain there in 2015. North of the signal box at Railway Cottages is a tramway, later part of the Ewesley Quarry Company. The signal box was actually a ground frame hut.

EWESLEY QUARRY

62. The Ewesley Quarry Company used three locomotives. No. 1 has been tentatively identified as Manning Wardle no. 495 of 1874 coming to Fontburn around 1900 and scrapped before 1937. No. 3 was an Andrew Barclay 0-4-0ST, their no. 1250 of 1911. This was for sale in 1938, but lay a long time until going for scrap. *Ewesley* no. 2, photographed here, was a Hawthorn Leslie 0-4-0ST no. 2496 of 1901, new to Ewesley and sold on to firms in Sunderland in its later life. (R.Jermy coll.)

FORESTBURNGATE

63. A very evocative shot of class G5 0-4-4T no. 67295 at Forestburngate with a one coach train for Rothbury. There was another quarry railway at Forestburngate, that took both stone and coal out by a ¾ mile long standard gauge line worked by *Wingate*, an Andrew Barclay 0-4-0ST, their no. 675 of 1891. Coal mining stopped in 1923, but quarrying may have used the mineral branch until about 1930. (E.E.Smith/R.W.Lynn coll.)

LEE SIDING

The first siding was opened in 1877 to receive coal from Lee Bridge Colliery, which closed in 1890. It was reopened about 1920 as a couple of short exchange sidings with loading docks fed by a double tramway from the Lee Pit, about ¾ miles to the southeast. The sidings were worked as required by up trains. The pit was damaged in the 1926 miners strike and the siding closed in 1927.

BRINKBURN HALT

XIV.   The station opened on 1st June 1904 at the end of a minor road. It comprised of the station, goods store and station masters house. The last remains as holiday accommodation. There was one siding in the goods yard, but close by was the base station of a two mile aerial ropeway, which brought coal from Healey Coote Colliery.

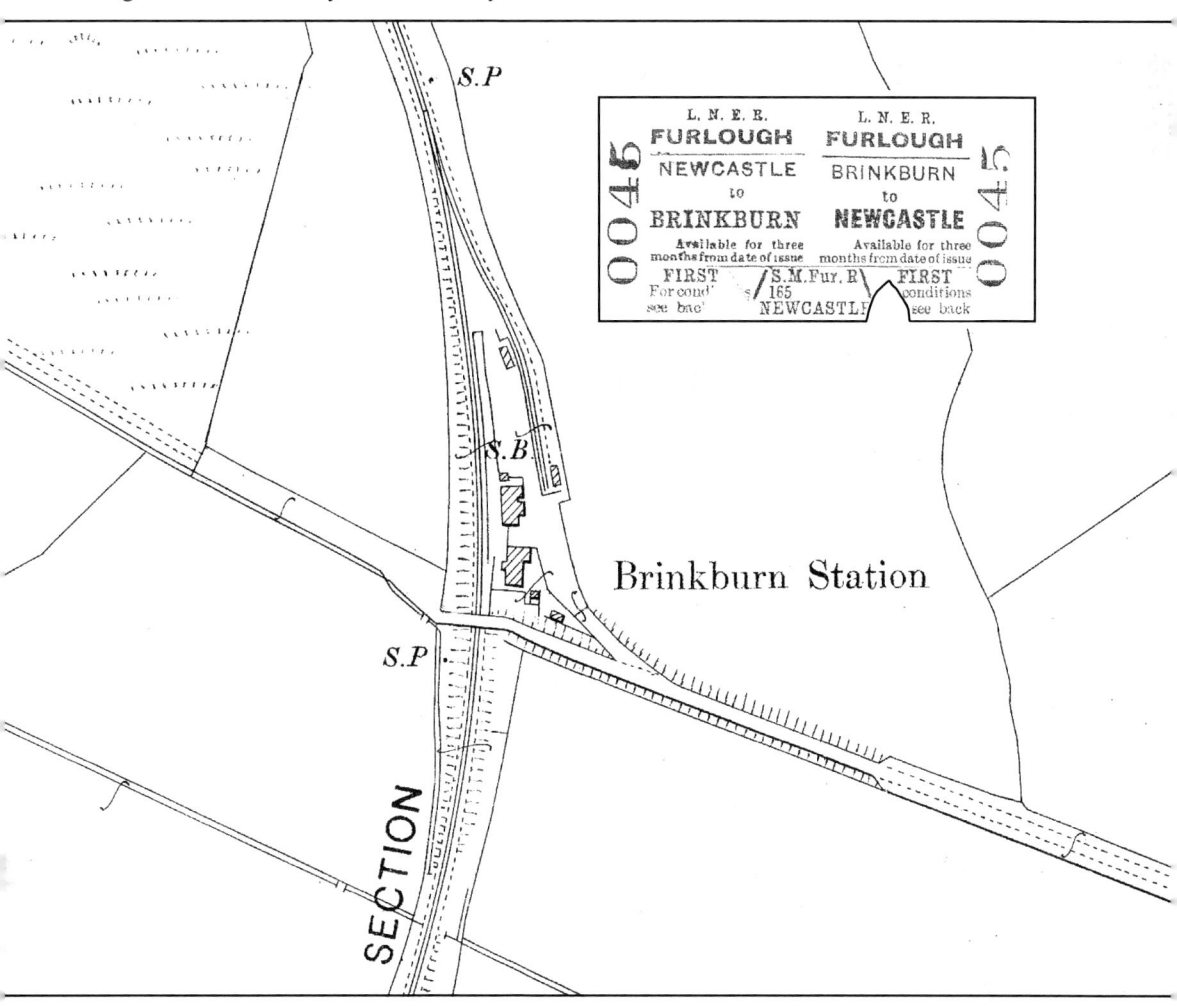

64. On 6th July 1951, G5 class 0-4-4T no. 67296 has pulled into Brinkburn station with the 5.50pm train bound for Rothbury. The wooden station building had vertical boarding; the goods shed was of corrugated iron. There was a ground frame in a hut. (W.A.Camwell/SLS)

65. Ten years later, on 25th June 1961, the passenger service has long gone but the arrival of a goods train hauled by J21 class 0-6-0 no. 65033, going south to Scotsgap is a source of interest to a youth group on a day out. (R.Montgomery)

66. A further two years and the line is about to close completely. By 14th June 1963, the station has lost its cared for look and the station master's cottage has been fenced off. (A.E.Young)

Despite closing half a century earlier, Brinkburn station is still signposted. It was seen here on 3rd September 2014. It was officially downgraded to a halt in BR (NE) days.
(D.A.Lovett)

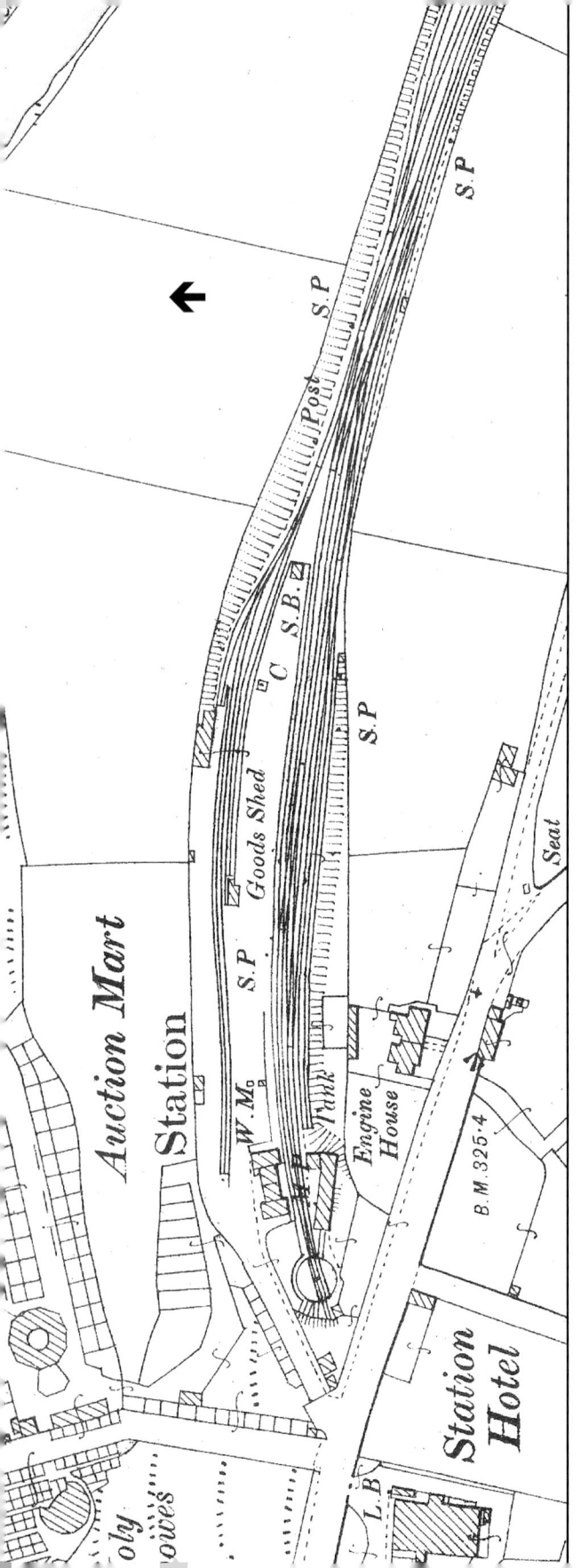

ROTHBURY

XV. The Northumberland Central Railway's original plan was to join up with the Berwick to Kelso line somewhere near Ford. In reaching Rothbury, they had only got halfway and the rather cramped station site, next to the auction mart on the south side of the town and the river, rather indicated they were not going to go any further.

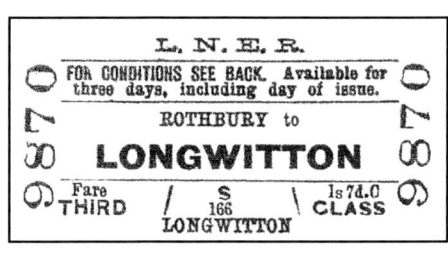

67. The station had a single platform with the platform track, run around loop and wooden engine shed accessed all from the turntable, from which this tinted postcard has been photographed. In the platform is a long train of NBR four wheel coaches. The length of the train suggests an excursion or race day special. On race days, passenger trains were also unloaded at the goods dock. There was some rebuilding of the station in 1899. (J.Alsop coll.)

68. Goods facilities and shunting, particularly for livestock trains were provided by quite a complicated system of points and three long sidings parallel to the running line. In 1905, an NBR E class (J31) 0-6-0 is at work. The large house in the middle distance is Cragside, the home of William Armstrong, inventor and industrialist. It was the first house in the world to be powered by hydro-electricity and is now part of the National Trust. (J.Alsop coll.)

69. The Rothbury branch led a quiet and uneventful life, but a very long and very late returning excursion to the pantomime at Newcastle resulted in this derailment when a point blade broke under the train when they were attempting to shunt the empty coaches into the goods dock siding. (R.W.Lynn coll.)

70. In October 1915, there was a fire inside the wooden engine shed and two Drummond C (J32) class locomotives inside were damaged. The need to use the turntable meant it was not possible to get them out. No. 487 was a Drummond M Class 4-4-0 (D28) named *Montrose,* sent to tow the two locomotives to Cowlairs Works in Glasgow. The shed was rebuilt in brick. (R.W.Lynn coll.)

71. The final regular passenger train, the 4.30pm for Morpeth leaves Rothbury on 13th September 1952 hauled by G5 class 0-4-4T no. 67341. (R.W.Lynn coll.)

72. Up until the early 1960s, there was sufficient goods traffic for the yard to maintain a road van feeder service. This is a BR Ford Thames lorry in the goods yard on 24th September 1961. (R.W.Lynn coll,)

73. This overall view of the station buildings, on 9th November 1963, probably involved a bit of scrambling on the photographer's part. (R.M.Casserley)

74. While 0-6-0 class J25 no. 65687 marshals its goods train, its safety valve steam nicely highlights the NBR signals. The signal box was opened in 1893, with 23 levers, and closed in 1963.(Colour-Rail.com)

75. J21 class 0-6-0 no. 65033 waits for the signalman and permission to leave for Scotsgap. The wooden construction next to the signal box is for token exchange, but this was not used after the end of passenger traffic. No. 65033 has led a charmed life and was being restored by Locomotive Conservation and Learning Trust. (Milepost 92½)

76. One of the last excursions on the branch used two four-coach class 101 DMUs and was on 24th July 1960. (Colour-Rail.com)

ROTHBURY ENGINE SHED

77. Two of the 30 Drummond R class 4-4-0Ts (later D51 class) were allocated to the branch and subshedded from Blaydon. From 1880 until 1884, no. 72 carried the name *Morpeth* and no. 73, seen here on the turntable in front of the shed, *Rothbury*. These were later renumbered 1401 and 1402 and withdrawn in 1925. A third member of the class, no. 103 *Montrose*, went to Newcastle for the Stephenson Jubilee Celebrations in 1881. (R.W.Lynn coll.)

78. J21 class 0-6-0 no. 65103 has come off its BR scenic excursion from Newcastle to Rothbury via Reedsmouth on 19th August 1956, and moved on to the turntable. (R.S.Carpenter)

79. The turntable has rail connections to the engine shed on the left, then the permanent way railcar in its tin shed, then for wagon supplies to Cowans & Oliver. (N.E.Stead)

80. This is another classic Rothbury shot with the station, locomotive, turntable and shed. What makes this picture different is that the locomotive is 4MT 2-6-0 no. 46474 and that the platelayer's Wickham Trolley is occupying the shed. (W.S.Sellar)

KNOWESGATE

XVI. We have left Rothbury and gone south across the moors to Scotsgap where we have rejoined the Wansbeck Valley line in its westward journey across more moorland to the hamlet of Knowesgate. Like Scotsgap, this was a strategic station at a road junction. There was a quarry 4½ miles to the northwest at Elsdon that had been worked for dressed stone since 1860. It had a tramway to the main road, but in 1904 a new lease was negotiated and in 1907-08 a 3ft gauge railway was built from Blaxter's Quarry to the goods platform at Knowesgate where a crane helped with transhipment.

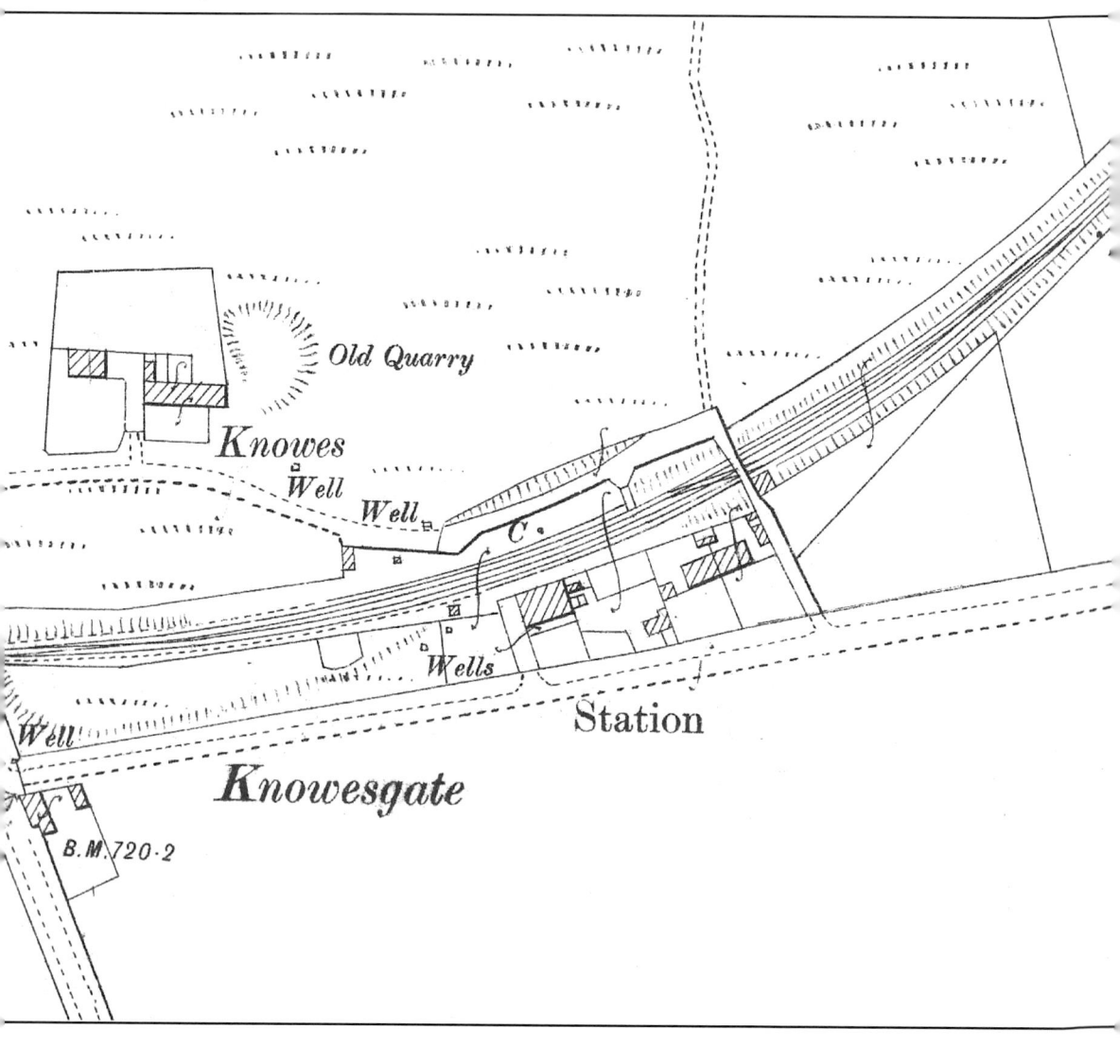

81. Looking east towards Scotsgap, this commercial postcard dates from about 1918. Besides showing the station buildings, it has captured the loading of cut stone from Blaxter's Quarry - and also the shadow of the photographer and his bulky camera! The station was opened as Knowes Gate (or Knowe's Gate) and renamed Knowesgate in January 1908. (J.Alsop coll.)

82. Cut blocks of architectural stone are being loaded from the goods dock. The narrow gauge line ran into the dock but no photographs of the locomotives or flat wagons on the dock have been found. In this view, the blocks are being unloaded from a flatbed lorry. (R.W.Lynn coll.)

83. This photograph from a passing train is looking to the west and shows the station gardens to good effect. Knowesgate was the station for Kirkwelphington, 1½ miles south with a population of 360. (J.W.Armstrong/ARPT)

84. Here we have a closer view of the station buildings. The station had a signal box with 38 levers from 1915 to 1924. This replaced a ground frame opened in 1893 and after closure of the box it was replaced by another ground frame after 1924. It remained a block post until 1959 with the instruments in the station office. In 2015, the buildings were still present, converted to private dwellings. The loading bank also survived in the undergrowth. (A.J.Wickens/ARPT)

85. J36 class 0-6-0 no. 9779 leaves Knowesgate with a train from Reedsmouth. This engine became BR no. 65331 and survived until August 1963. The passenger service ceased on 15th September 1952 and the freight service on 3rd October 1963. (R.W.Lynn coll.)

Bradshaw's Timetable for July 1938.

BLAXTER QUARRY RAILWAY

86. The first locomotive to work on the railway was 0-4-0ST *Ottercops*. Another locomotive *Mary* 0-4-0ST W. Bagnall no. 1717 of 1903 was hired, but in 1912 a third locomotive was bought, another Hudswell Clarke 0-4-0ST pictured here hauling flat wagons with stones on them. This was *Blaxter* no. 971 of 1912. The fate of the narrow gauge line is uncertain, but seems to have been out of use by 1930. In 1928, a standard gauge line operated within the confines of the quarry worked by an Atkinson - Walker 4wVBT no. 113 of 1928. It ran until 1940, when the quarry temporarily ceased work. (Bellingham Heritage Centre/N.R.O. Woodhorn)

XVII. A map of the Blaxter Quarry Railway in 1910. (A.E.Young)

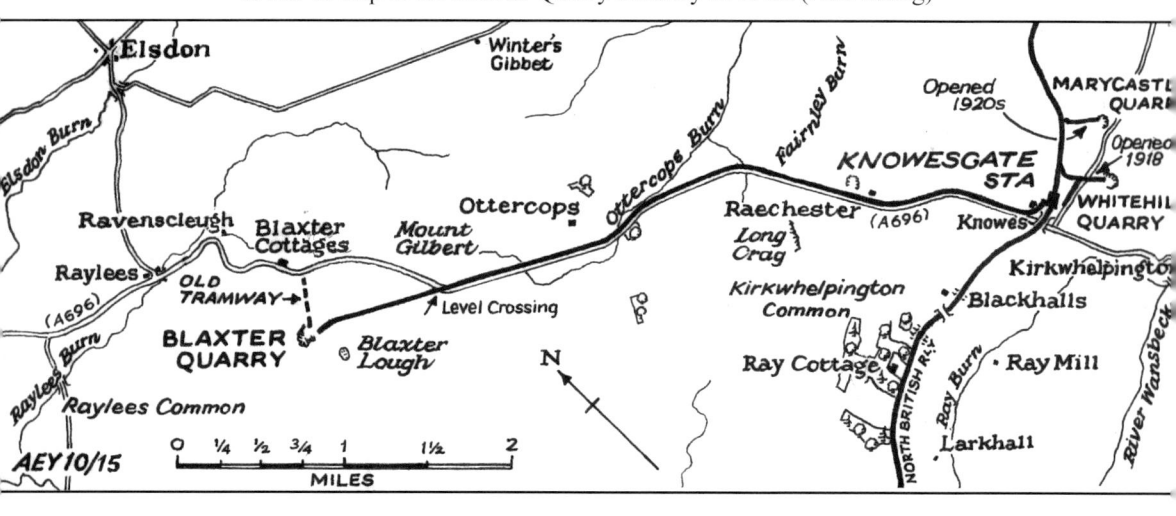

RAY HOUSE

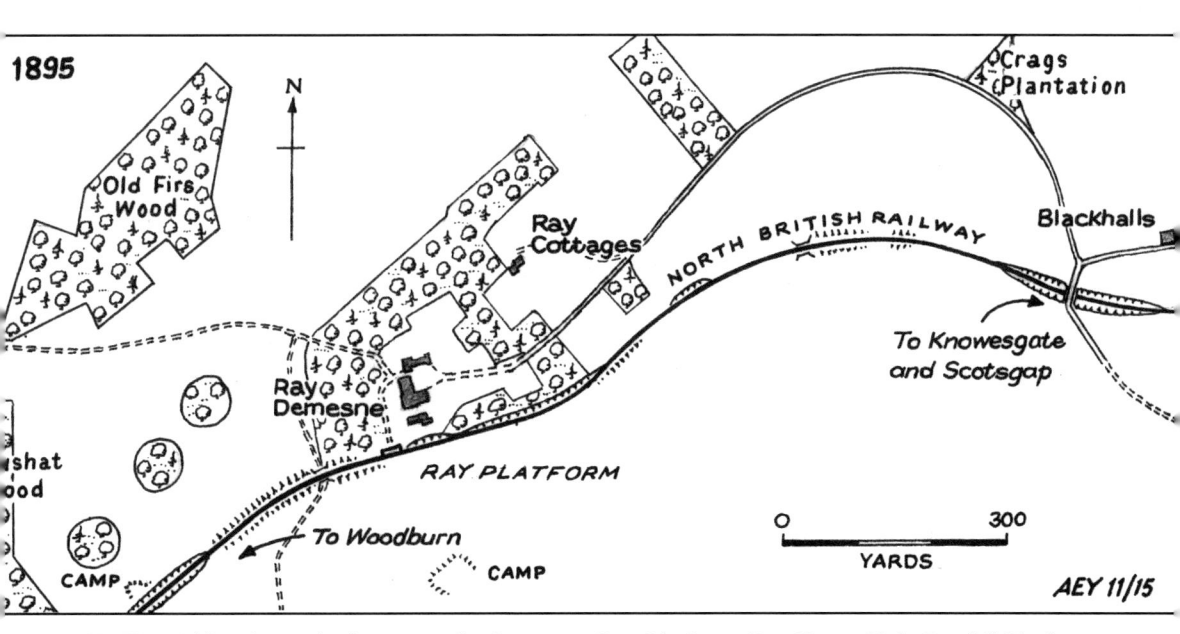

XVIII. This private platform was also known as Ray Platform, Ray House Halt, Rayfell Platform or Parsons Platform (LNER). It served the Ray Demesne Estate, which was owned from 1905 by Sir C.A.Parsons, the Tyneside industrialist. He invented the steam turbine; his firm at Heaton specialised in turbo generators and electrical engineering. He used the platform from the early 1900s until his death on 11th February 1931 and Estate staff continued to use it afterwards. During his lifetime there was a special mail delivery via Reedsmouth by the up morning train and a collection via Morpeth, by the afternoon up train. Everyone else got their mail by road from Kirkwelphington Post Office. The Ray Demesne house passed to the Government in 1947 and was demolished shortly afterwards. In the grounds is a ruined Bastle, a fortified farmhouse where the cattle could be kept on the ground floor and the people above. The last use of the platform was thought to be 1949. (A.E.Young)

SUMMIT COTTAGES

87. Summit Cottages are at an altitude of 815ft and are appropriately named. A class J27 0-6-0 is about to pass them with a freight for Scotsgap and Morpeth. The cottages still exist as holiday homes but by 2015, the hillside was covered with a mature conifer plantation. (R.W.Lynn coll.)

88. Summit Cottages was an unofficial station (on Fridays it was official!) for local people with steps carried in the guard's compartment to allow them to get on and off the train. J21 class 0-6-0 no. 65105 has approached the summit. Behind, the view is downhill across Stiddlehill Common to Woodburn. Until 1866 there was a siding linked to a tramway to Stiddlehill drift mine. (R.W.Lynn coll.)

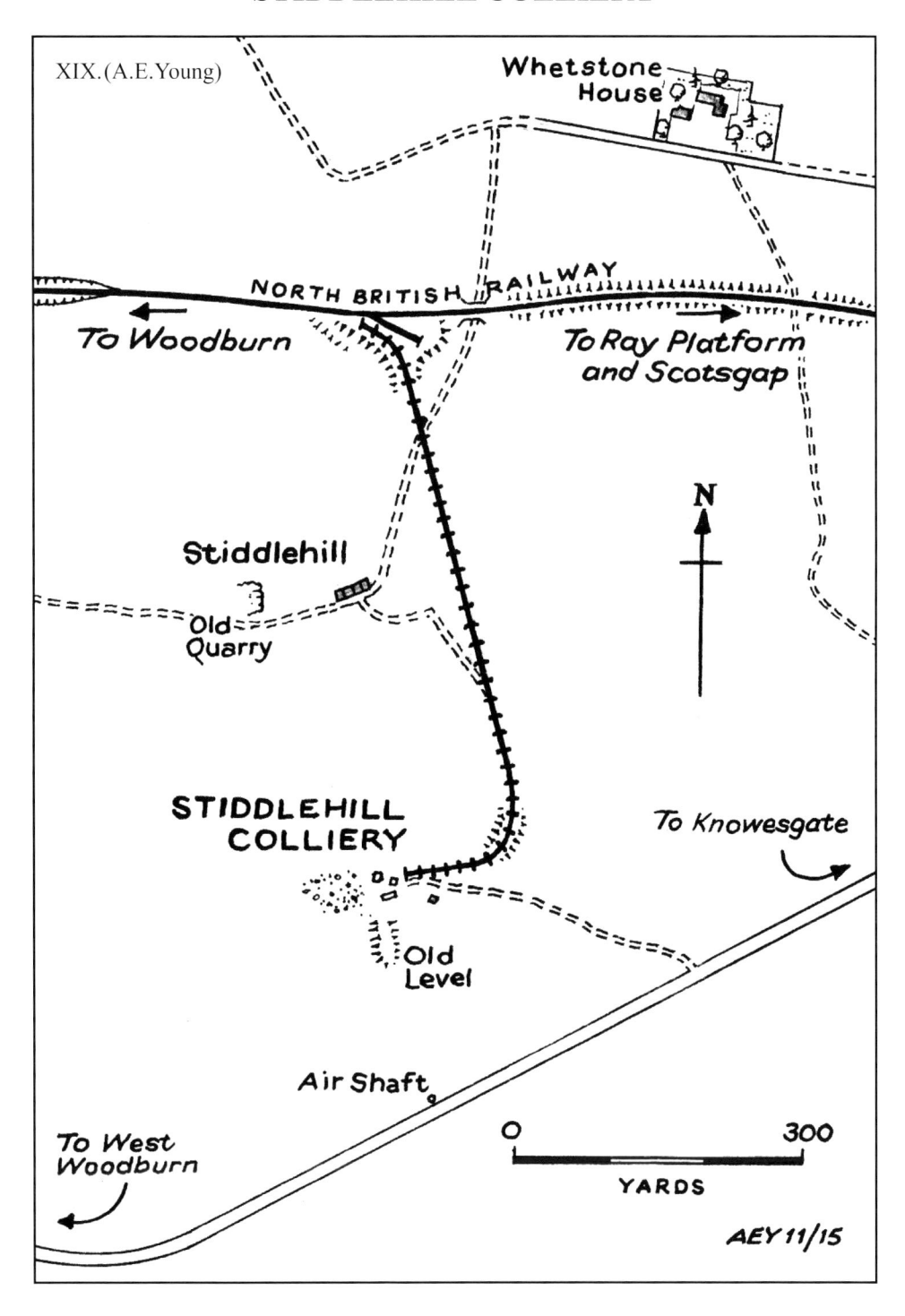

STIDDLEHILL COLLIERY

XIX.(A.E.Young)

Whetstone House

NORTH BRITISH RAILWAY

To Woodburn

To Ray Platform and Scotsgap

N

Stiddlehill
Old Quarry

STIDDLEHILL COLLIERY

To Knowesgate

Old Level

Air Shaft

To West Woodburn

0　　　300
YARDS

AEY 11/15

WOODBURN

XX. The arc of the station site included two quarries with narrow gauge tracks that led to interchange sidings. Parkside Quarry was on the south side of the road and was worked from 1880 to about 1920. Station Quarry originally transhipped closer to the station as shown here but after 1925 unloaded at the loop east of the station. The station was the railhead for the Otterburn Army Training Area, which opened in 1911 and still trains about 30,000 soldiers a year.

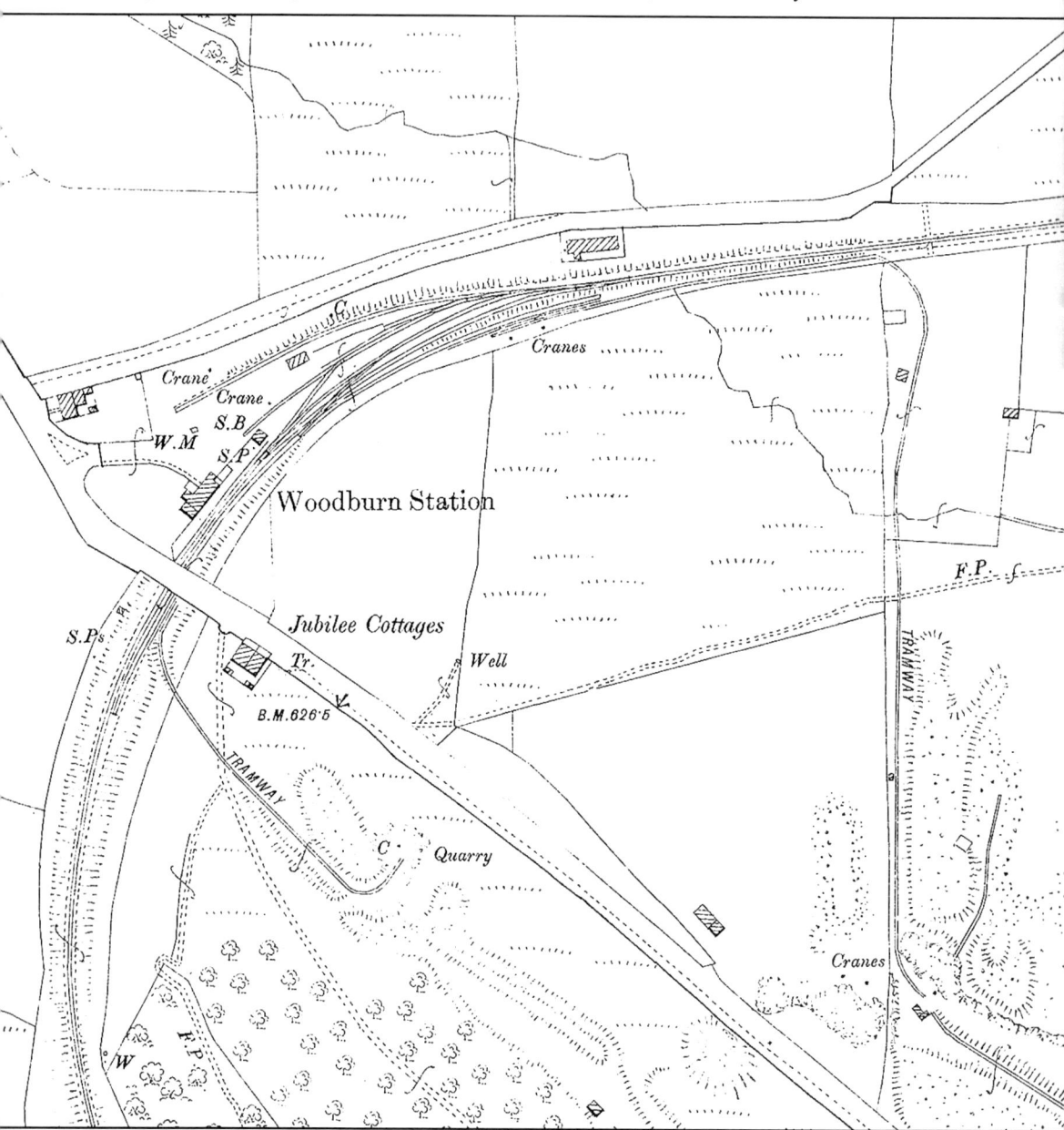

89. The single storey station, with its curved platform and fairly large goods yard served the scattered cottages of West and East Woodburn, Chesterhope and Risdale. It was also the railhead for various military ranges in the area and whilst the line west of Woodburn closed on 11th November 1963, Woodburn remained open until 3rd October 1966. (J.Alsop coll.)

90. A military train arrives with men and horses from the Royal Field Artillery for a training camp out on the range. The cattle trucks used for the horses were disinfected with lime. That is why the vehicles are white. The railway company charged extra for limed wagons! All the stock is NBR which suggests a Scottish contingent of soldiers. (R.W.Lynn coll.)

91. This is the entrance to the goods yard and most of the people are in civilian dress or railway uniform, but doubtless they are waiting to see the military trot up the road to the camp. (R.W.Lynn coll.)

Otterburn Training Camp

There are two target railways known to have been on the range. The Silloans or Sills Target Railway was 2ft 6ins gauged and powered vehicles towed targets to where they were required. The White Spot Target Railway is ⅓ mile of elevated metre gauge track that used a petrol unit to tow the targets.

92. Here the 67th Royal Field Artillery are collecting their horses. The soldier leading the first horse appears to be carrying a ceremonial harness. Could it be that the large black dog is the 67th's mascot? (R.W.Lynn coll.)

93. Moving through time to the winter of 1947, the worst winter of the 20th century, we find that between Woodburn and Scotsgap the line was well and truly blocked with snow. So much snow that a double-ended two engine snowplough like this one with two class J27 0-6-0 was abandoned for a time.
(R.W.Lynn coll.)

94. The double plough was hard at work in February 1947. Keeping the line clear was so difficult that the Worcester Gas Turbine Company put two inclined Whittle jet engines mounted side by side on a four wheel wagon. This was not a success - it did melt the snow but it also blew away the ballast! It was tried at Woodburn on 20th March 1947. (R.W.Lynn coll.)

95. Woodburn yard and station is viewed from the east as class J27 0-6-0 no. 65882 shunts the day's freight. The signal box opened in 1893 with 32 levers and closed in 1966. (R.W.Lynn coll.)

96. A diesel multiple unit excursion led by a class 104 set enters Woodburn, with the signalman collecting the token. The styling was called "Cats Whiskers". (R.W.Lynn coll.)

97. It is July 1965 and this small 0-4-0DM *Andy* J.Fowler no. 16038 of 1923 was in Woodburn goods yard to assist with the recovery of track and materials. There are a couple of NBR vans in the background. *Andy* was Fowler's first petrol locomotive and survives at the Midland Railway Centre. (R.R.Darsley)

98. Woodburn had its busy times and its challenges. To construct a dam at Catcleugh near Byrness, some 16 miles from Woodburn, a 3ft gauge railway was laid down, beginning in 1891. For the early construction this Dunbar & Ruston steam navvy has been delivered in three parts to Woodburn. The 3ft gauge line started from Woodburn with an incline so it is unlikely the navvy made the journey on the railway, but traction engines hauled it up the road probably destroying the road surface as they went. Quite a problem for the station agent. (R.W.Lynn coll.)

CATCLEUGH RESERVOIR

The Newcastle & Gateshead Water Company built an earth dam in the Rede Valley, three miles south of the Scottish border. This created a lake, 1½ miles long and about 2,300 million gallons capacity. The project began in 1889. The first part was to lay a 30 inch diameter pipe from Catcleugh, 27 miles to Colt Crag, Woodford Bridge near Barrasford and thence join an existing pipeline to Wylam. From Woodburn to Woodford Bridge there were temporary 3ft gauge railways built to get the pipeline constructed, but by 1895 a more permanent line was built from Woodburn to Catcleugh to carry all the materials for the construction site. While there were not many cuttings or embankments, there were substantial trestle bridges, the largest being the viaduct over Big Burn, south of Otterburn. The standard gauge sidings at Woodburn were extended by the NBR in 1898-99, particularly for the carriage of cement which was transhipped to the 3ft line.

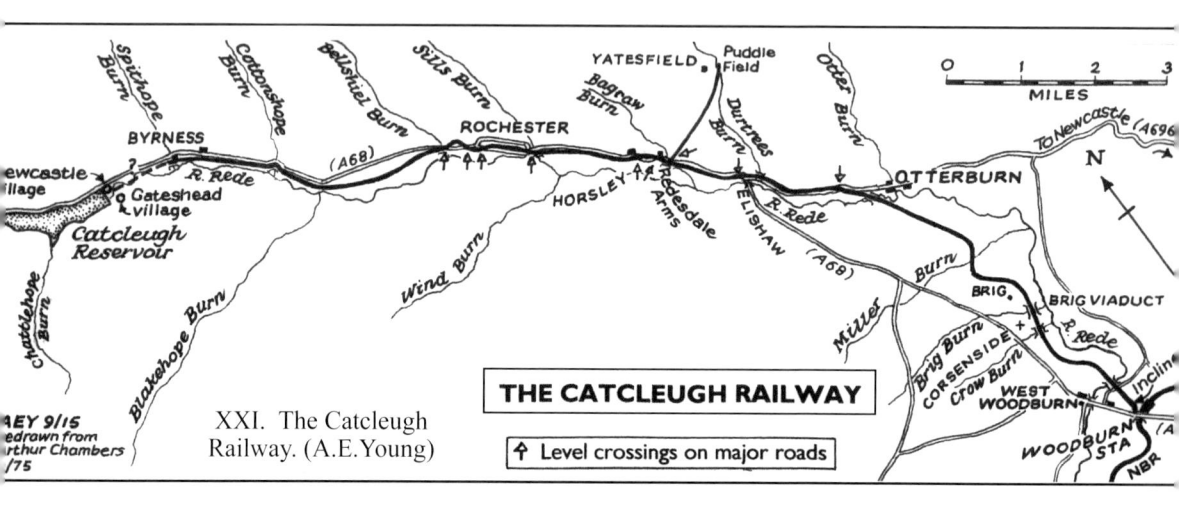

XXI. The Catcleugh Railway. (A.E.Young)

In 1902, the tramway hauled 49,166 tons. Construction workers lived in hutted villages either side of the Rede which were known as Newcastle (on the north bank) and Gateshead (on the south). There were about 50 huts, a hospital, a surgery, a canteen, a post office, a guild room, a navvy mission and a policeman. At the peak in April 1899, there were 331 men, 79 women and 94 children. The older children went to school in Byrness. There are two memorial windows in Byrness church to the 64 people who died in the villages from accidents or natural causes in the 10 years they existed. One of the huts survives as a museum to the site. The main problems were with the weather, floods and snow; with snow arriving in September 1898!

The valve closing ceremony was on 21st June 1904 and the lake filled by January 1906. The Catcleugh Railway closed on 13th May 1905 with the last recovery of materials in 1906. Surplus plant was sold off at the two sales at Woodburn station, on 26th July 1904 and 10th May 1905. While the 3ft gauge railway only lasted 10 years, at 16 miles in length it was longer than Scotsgap to Rothbury.

Locomotives at Catcleugh (all 3ft gauge)

Otterburn	0-4-0ST	Hudswell Clarke no. 418 of 1894
Catcleugh	0-4-0ST	Hudswell Clarke no. 423 of 1894
Woodburn	0-4-0ST	Hudswell Clarke no. 505 of 1899
Byrness	0-4-0ST	Hudswell Clarke no. 507 of 1899
Bruckless	0-4-0ST	Hunslet no. 564 of 1892
Whittle	0-4-0T	Black Hawthorn no. 588 of c.1880
Heugh	0-4-0ST	Hudswell Clarke no. 419 of 1894
Brig	0-4-0ST	Hudswell Clarke no. 504 of 1899
Ramshope	0-4-0ST	Hudswell Clarke no. 506 of 1899
Rede	0-4-0ST	W.G.Bagnall no. 1413 of 1894
Minnie	0-4-0ST	W.G.Bagnall no. 1426 of 1894

99. This is the main road to Scotland, now the A68, half a mile north of Otterburn where the A696 joins it. The Catcleugh railway, on the left, now follows the road closely. It is obvious why the water company decided to build a railway rather than use traction engines on the road. (Northumbrian Water Ltd.)

100. There was a self-acting incline from Woodburn station to just before the Rede river crossing, where the locomotives took over. There was a semi-official 'Paddy's Mail' with workmen sitting on wagons. A permit to travel was issued for people travelling at their own risk. School children travelled in the locomotive cab on wet school days. There was an official saloon, pictured here with *Brigg* 0-4-0ST Hudswell Clarke no. 504 of 1899. This was for the use of Charles Henzell, the company engineer who lived at Catcleugh House. Another van was also available for other passengers who had to leave the train in the meadow north of the Rede crossing and walk through the village to Woodburn station. (Northumbrian Water Ltd.)

101. 0-4-0ST *Otterburn* Hudswell Clarke no. 418 of 1894 is posed on the trestle viaduct over Crow Burn, some two miles up the line from Woodburn. In the foreground is the 30 inch diameter water pipe, halfway up the abutments. On the skyline is Corsenside church.
(Northumbrian Water Ltd.)

102. 0-4-0ST *Otterburn* at a later date has wooden windshields fitted to the cab and is towing timber bogies and a flat wagon. It is crossing Spithope burn, a mile south of Catcleugh. The pipeline is in the foreground. In the black hut museum there are couple of early skateboards used by boys sent down inside the pipe to clear out the silt. A rope was attached to haul them back to the entry point. (Northumbrian Water Ltd.)

103. However it got up to Catcleugh, the Dunbar & Ruston steam navvy got there. It was one of three on site. Horse drawn spoil wagons were used at the clay face of the puddle field on the Yatesfield branch. (Northumbrian Water Ltd.)

104. This looks like an official inspection part up on the spillway of the dam. The smaller steam cranes are in the background for lifting the stone blocks. The spillway is so constructed that any overflow spreads to an equal depth as it comes down to rejoin the River Rede at the base of the dam. The water company has to guarantee a given volume of water in the Rede to protect the fishing interests. The dressed stone spillway is 2,050ft long and 210ft wide. (Northumbrian Water Ltd.)

105. This is a view of the 'Newcastle' hutted camp from the 'Gateshead' side. The main railway crosses the River Rede from the left. The long hut in the foreground is the Navvy Mission's Hall. The trestle bridge stone bases are still there and the preserved hut is on the left hand side back row. (Northumbrian Water Ltd.)

106. This is the surviving hut from 1895-1905. It was lived in by George Milburn and his family until 1926 when it was used as a store and office until 1945 and then forgotten. In 1988, a campaign to save it was successful and it was restored and placed on proper foundations. Half of the building is a house and the other half a store and office. Equipment was left in as at 1926. The original families have been traced and they have given original furnishings and fittings. The hut belongs to Northumbrian Water but the first Sunday afternoon of the Summer months there is a guided tour led by Northumberland Park Rangers. (R.R.Darsley)

107. It is time to go back down the railway to Woodburn. This is a Sunday School outing with *Otterburn* leading the train and a second locomotive and, possibly, train behind. The story is that the children went for a day at the seaside at Newbiggin by the Sea. This would be feasible but a long day! Catcleugh, Woodburn, Morpeth, Ashington to Newbiggin - and then all the way back! (Northumbrian Water Ltd.)

We shall leave the narrow gauge at Woodburn and go west on our way to Reedsmouth.

1952 - The final timetable before closure.

Table 76 MORPETH, SCOTSGAP and REEDSMOUTH and ROTHBURY

Miles			WEEKDAYS am	am	pm	pm	
	3 Newcastle	dep	9 28	....	5 6	....	....
—	**MORPETH**	dep	**10 10**	..	**5 50**	..	..
5½	Meldon	,,	10 22	....	6 3	....	....
7¾	Angerton	,,	10 29	..	6 9	..	..
9¼	Middleton North	,,	10 34	....	6 14	....	....
11¼	**Scotsgap** (for Cambo)	arr	**10 40**	..	**6 20**	..	..
—	**Scotsgap** (for Cambo)	dep	....	**10 46**	....	**6 27**	....
14¾	Knowesgate	,,	..	10 55	..	6 38	..
21½	Woodburn	,,	....	11 8	....	6 52	....
25¼	**Reedsmouth**	arr	..	**11 15**	..	**7 0**	..
—	**Scotsgap** (for Cambo)	dep	**10 43**	....	**6 22**	....	....
14½	Longwitton	,,	10 52	..	6 31	..	..
16½	Ewesley	,,	10 57	....	6 38	....	....
17½	Fontburn Halt	,,	11 2	..	6 43	..	..
22	Brinkburn Halt	,,	11 12	....	6A52	....	....
24¼	**ROTHBURY**	arr	**11 18**	..	**6 58**	..	..

Miles			WEEKDAYS am	am	pm Bellingham (dep 4.5 pm)	pm	
—	**ROTHBURY**	dep	..	**7 51**		**4 30**	..
2¼	Brinkburn Halt	,,	....	7 56		4 35	....
6½	Fontburn Halt	,,	..	8 7		4 46	..
7¾	Ewesley	,,	....	8 10		4 49	....
9¾	Longwitton	,,	..	8 16		4 55	..
13	**Scotsgap** (for Cambo)	arr	....	**8 22**		**5 1**	....
—	**Reedsmouth**	dep	**7 44**	..	**4 15**	..	..
3¾	Woodburn	,,	7 54	....	4 24	....	....
10½	Knowesgate	,,	8 9	..	4 39	..	..
14	**Scotsgap** (for Cambo)	arr	**8 18**	....	**4 48**	....	....
—	**Scotsgap** (for Cambo)	dep	..	**8 25**	..	**5 2**	..
15	Middleton North	,,	....	8 29	....	5 6	....
16½	Angerton	,,	..	8 34	..	5 10	..
18¾	Meldon	,,	....	8 40	....	5 15	....
24¼	**MORPETH**	arr	..	**8 51**	..	**5 25**	..
40¾	3 Newcastle	arr	....	9 29	....	6 11	....

A—Calls to set down only.

CRAIG QUARRY SIDING

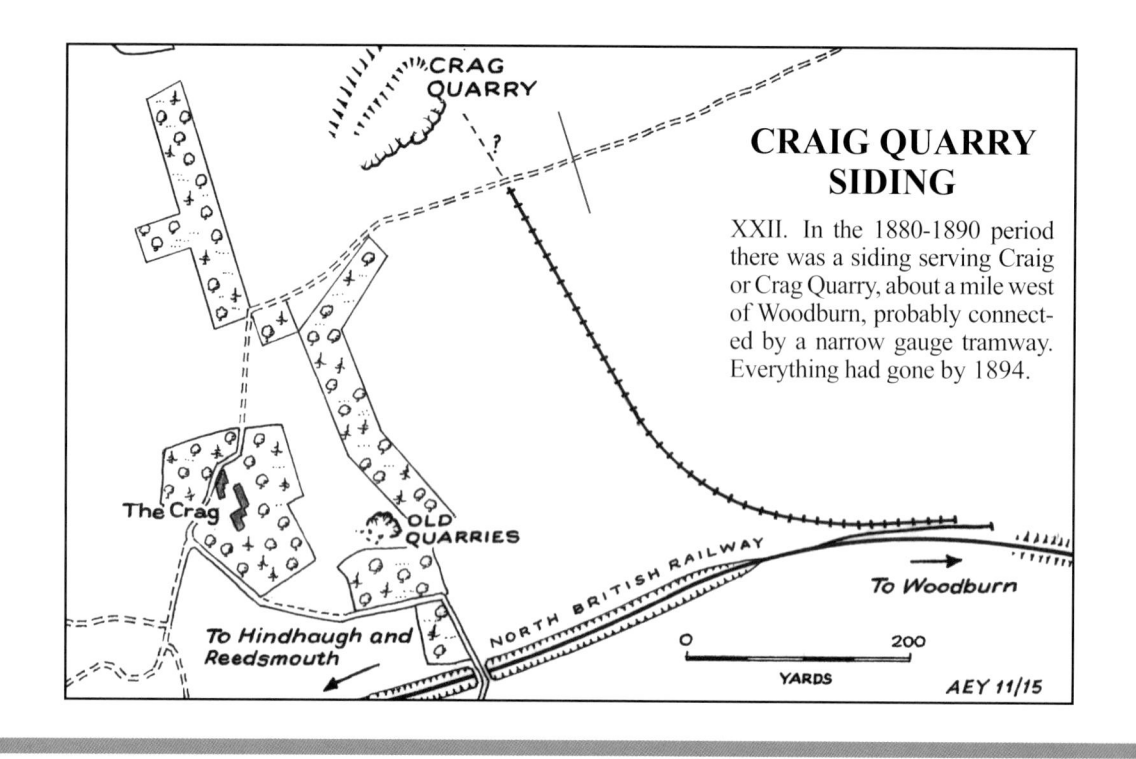

XXII. In the 1880-1890 period there was a siding serving Craig or Crag Quarry, about a mile west of Woodburn, probably connected by a narrow gauge tramway. Everything had gone by 1894.

HINDHAUGH PLATFORM

XXIII. Some 1200 yards north of Broomhope Junction were large iron ore kilns about 200ft long set into the hillside and top fed by a tramway bringing the ore from the iron ore workings around Ridsdale. There was a 150 yard loop with a 55 yard loading dock. Interestingly, in the early days an average of about 120 tickets were sold from Bellingham to Hindhaugh. There was no convenient return working so the workers walked home. The kilns closed in 1879 and have been demolished, but the workers return path remains running from nowhere to nowhere!

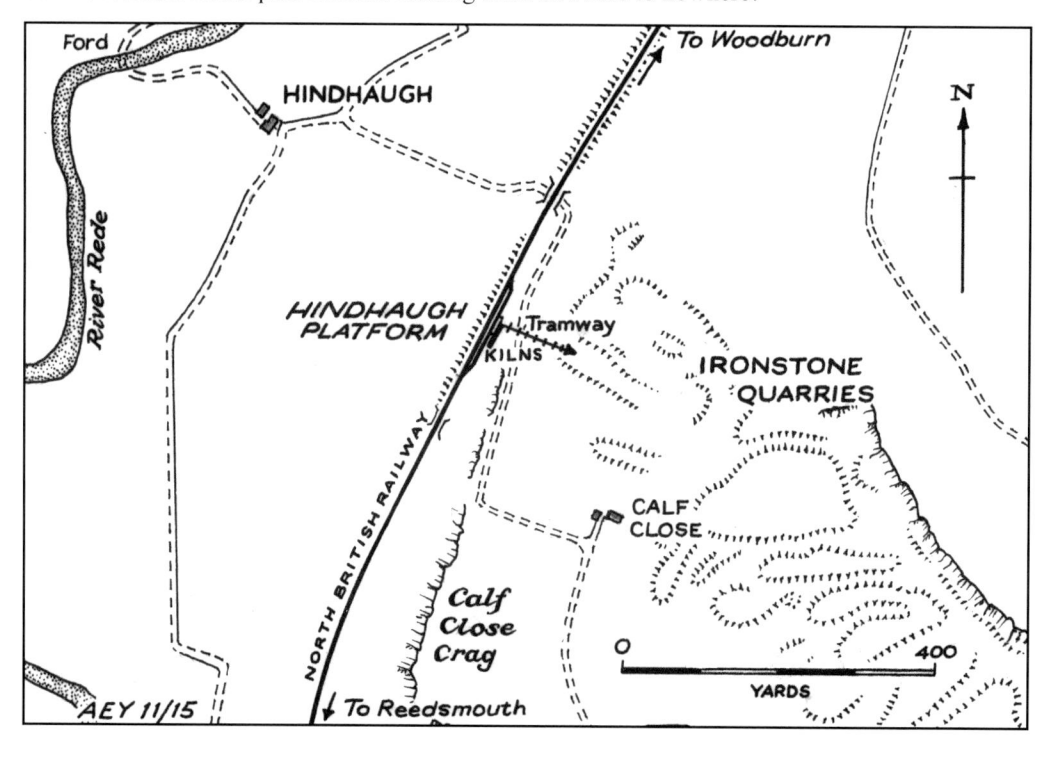

BROOMHOPE SIDING

Iron Ore workings at Broomhope and Hindhaugh were restarted in 1864 by Sir W.G. Armstrong to supply his engineering works at Elswick. These workings closed in 1879 after the extraction of over half a million tons of ore and limestone. Armstrong retained ownership and established an armaments testing area in the Broomhope Valley which was and still is closed to the public. In the 1880s, two test bunkers were in use and by the 1920s this was increased to five. Each bunker was surrounded by earth banks with separate rail access and a rail-mounted overhead gantry crane for lifting the larger naval guns. The NER had special wagons based on pairs of six wheel tender frames permanently coupled and able to carry 32 tons. Two of these were used for each gun, one having the breach cradle and the other supporting the muzzle.

The LNER built wagons based on Great Central diamond frame bogies - six of these could take a load of 140 tons for the 14 to 16 inch guns of World War II. Small to medium guns were carried on ordinary flat wagons or machinery trucks. The larger gun sets were worked as special trains and were double headed to Reedsmouth. The Broomhope branch was always worked by main line locomotives; often the Reedsmouth pilot locomotive delivering on its own. Vickers Armstrong had small engine sheds in the valley and must have had their own shunting locomotives on site but no records have yet been found.

The assistance of trains from the rear was severely limited by the LNER and Reedsmouth to Broomhope was one place it was allowed, but the assisting locomotives had to be coupled to the train. Some of the military movements during the war were secret and rail staff had to sign the Official Secrets Act!

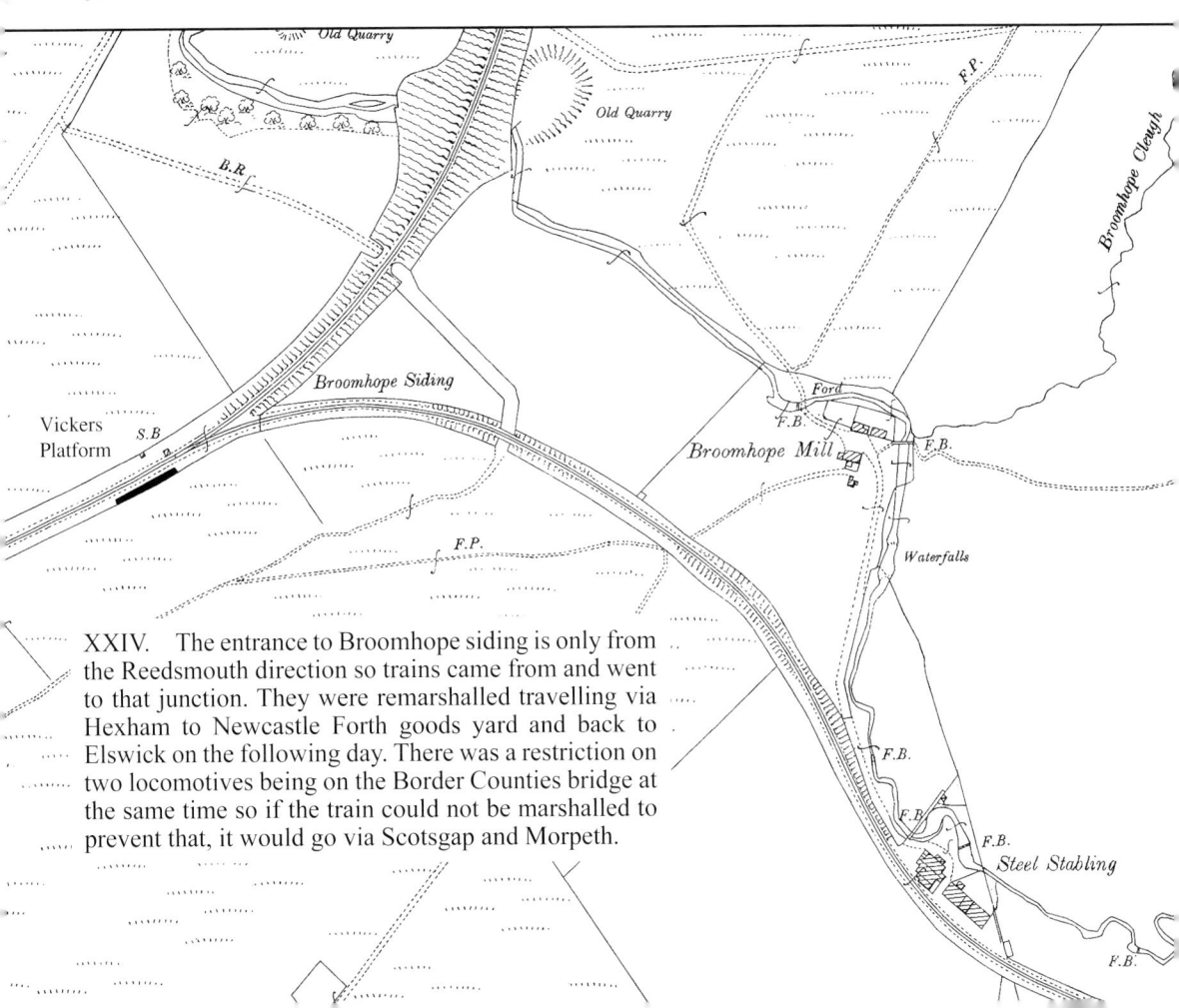

XXIV. The entrance to Broomhope siding is only from the Reedsmouth direction so trains came from and went to that junction. They were remarshalled travelling via Hexham to Newcastle Forth goods yard and back to Elswick on the following day. There was a restriction on two locomotives being on the Border Counties bridge at the same time so if the train could not be marshalled to prevent that, it would go via Scotsgap and Morpeth.

108. J25 class 0-6-0 no. 65727 has left its train on the main line and has gone down to Broomhope to fetch a van. It is now leaving with the fireman prepared to close the gates after it. (J.Spencer Gilks)

109. A photograph of a large gun for a ship enters the testing complex at Steel in LNER days. The train has a J21 class 0-6-0 no. 1564 at this end and another J21 at the other. It appears to be using the NER wagons. (M.Halbert)

110. Gun carrying wagons were known as gun sets to distinguish them from rail-mounted guns. The NER's largest gun set was this 60 ton articulated unit seen at Stooperdale, Darlington. In 1938, the LNER built two 140 ton carriers nos. 231273/4, one of which lasted until 1964.
(J.F.Mallon/Darlington Railway Museum)

VICKERS PLATFORM

Vickers platform was built of wood and was 130ft long. It was situated immediately on the southwest side of the line, south of the Broomhope points. The signal box opposite was actually a ground frame in a hut. Latterly, the two remaining point levers were placed at the end of the platform. The platform was opened in the 1900s and was used by Vickers Armstrong's staff and local people, tickets being issued to the station before the platform in either direction.

The passenger service closure notice consigns both branch lines towards their ultimate fate.
(R.W.Lynn coll.)

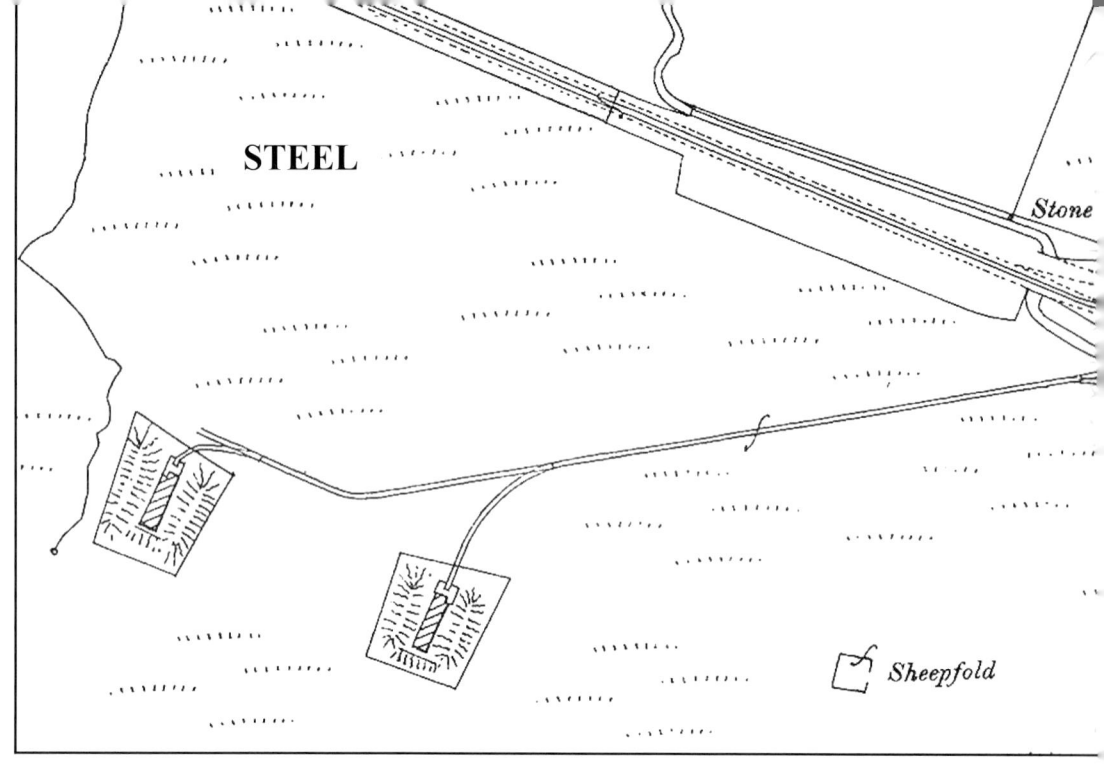

111. A view of Steel has two guns under the gantry crane. There appears to be a steam engine in front of the left-hand large shed with two breakdown cranes on the right and a small diesel locomotive on the bend. In the left foreground there is a narrow gauge tramway with a V-skip wagon on it. Elswick was the Vickers Armstrong munitions factory on the Tyne. Over the years, it had around 30 small shunting engines in the form of 0-4-0STs and 0-4-0Crane Tanks, more than half from Hawthorn Leslie. In 1958, it purchased three 4wDM from F.Hibberd. It is possible that shunting at the Steel site was done by locomotives transferred from Elswick. (R.W.Lynn coll.)

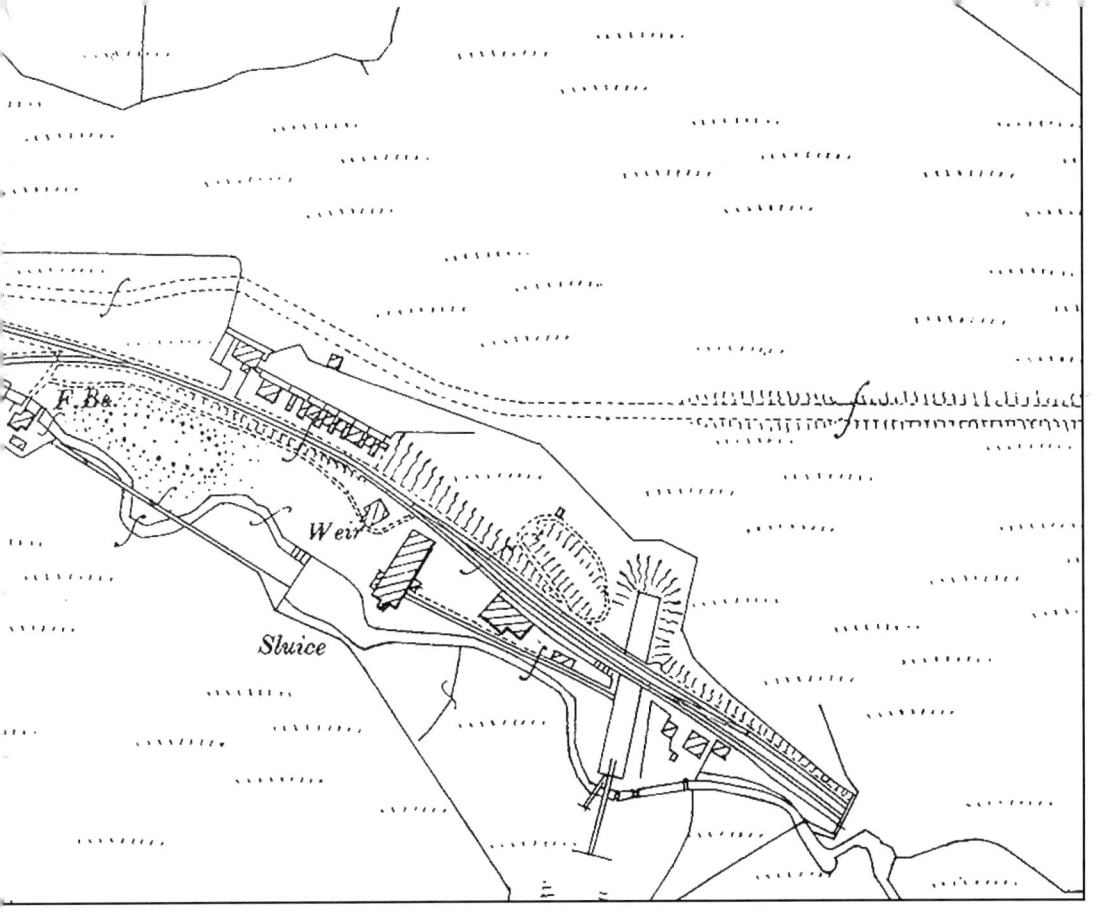

XXV. This is the continuation of map XXIV and shows the two test bunkers of the 1880s. The three later bunkers were built in the southern foreground of the map.

112. A large naval gun is in position for test firing on a very wet day, 13th March 1911. A standard gauge rail track goes into the bunker opening, but it appears the projectile is fired into the bunker. (Tyne & Wear Museum Archives)

113. A naval gun is in the act of firing. (Bellingham Heritage Centre)

114. J27 class 0-6-0 no. 65819 is returning from Steel. (M.Halbert coll.)

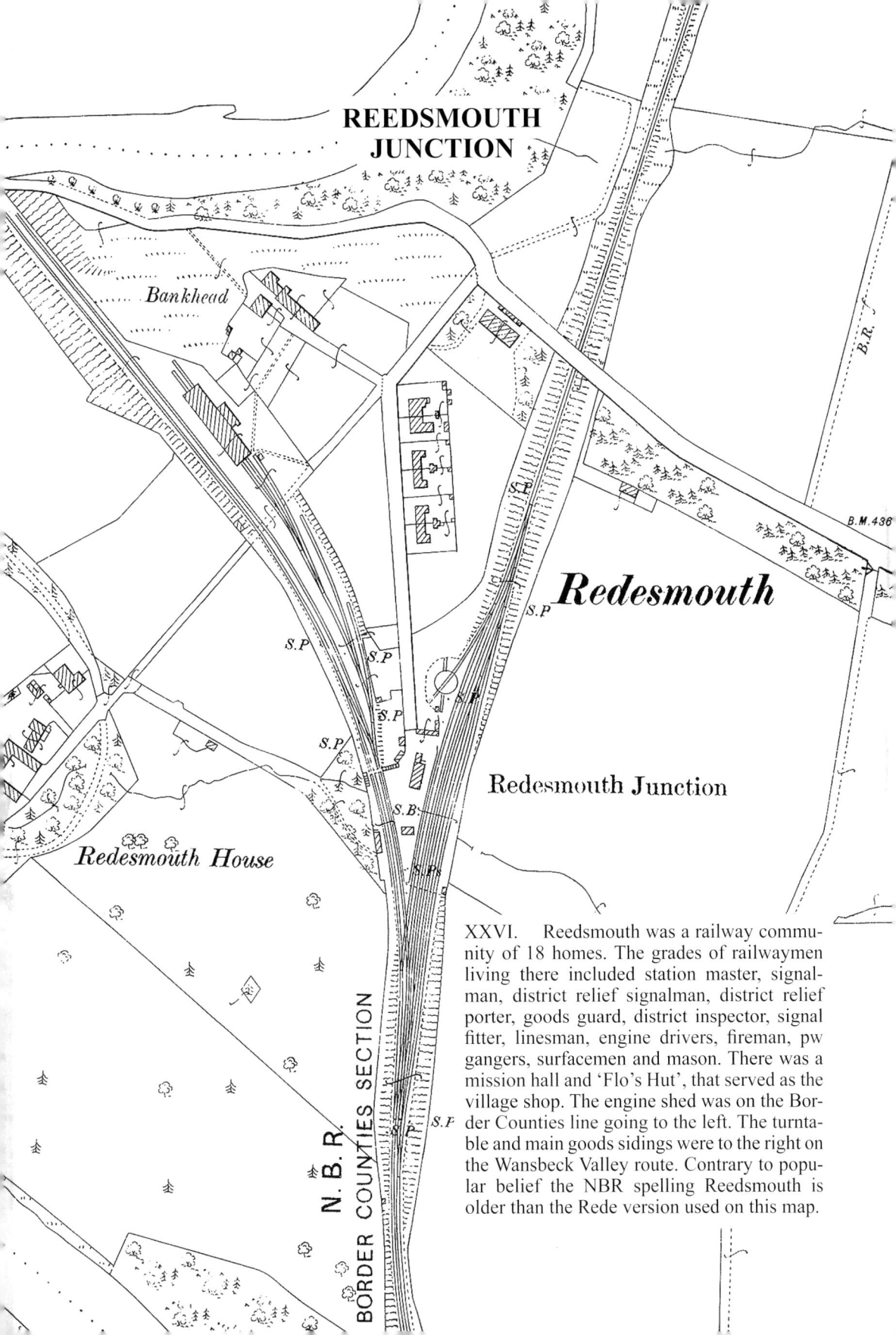

XXVI. Reedsmouth was a railway community of 18 homes. The grades of railwaymen living there included station master, signalman, district relief signalman, district relief porter, goods guard, district inspector, signal fitter, linesman, engine drivers, fireman, pw gangers, surfacemen and mason. There was a mission hall and 'Flo's Hut', that served as the village shop. The engine shed was on the Border Counties line going to the left. The turntable and main goods sidings were to the right on the Wansbeck Valley route. Contrary to popular belief the NBR spelling Reedsmouth is older than the Rede version used on this map.

115. This view of the station is dated about 1920. The signal box has got a second storey to improve the signalman's view. The station waiting rooms are under the very large water tank. Both buildings have been converted into residential use, though the water tank was replaced by a more conventional roof. (J.Alsop coll.)

116. J21 class 0-6-0 no. 65103 runs around its train, a summer gardens special, at Reedsmouth station. The train will proceed to Scotsgap and Morpeth. In the sidings behind the locomotive is a train full of field guns. (K.Hoole)

117. Another J21 class 0-6-0 no. 65042 is waiting to depart from Reedsmouth with the one coach train, the 4.15pm for Scotsgap. (K.Hoole)

REEDSMOUTH SHED

118. The 1862 NBR shed was off the Border Counties Line. Class V1 2-6-2T no. 67639 is waiting to leave Reedsmouth on a Saturday train to Kielder. The two road shed with its cantilevered roofed coaling plant was to standard NBR design. Three engines were usually allocated to the shed. During the 1939-45 war, five locomotives from the York Railway Museum were stored there. The building still survives in agricultural use. (I.S.Carr/ARPT)

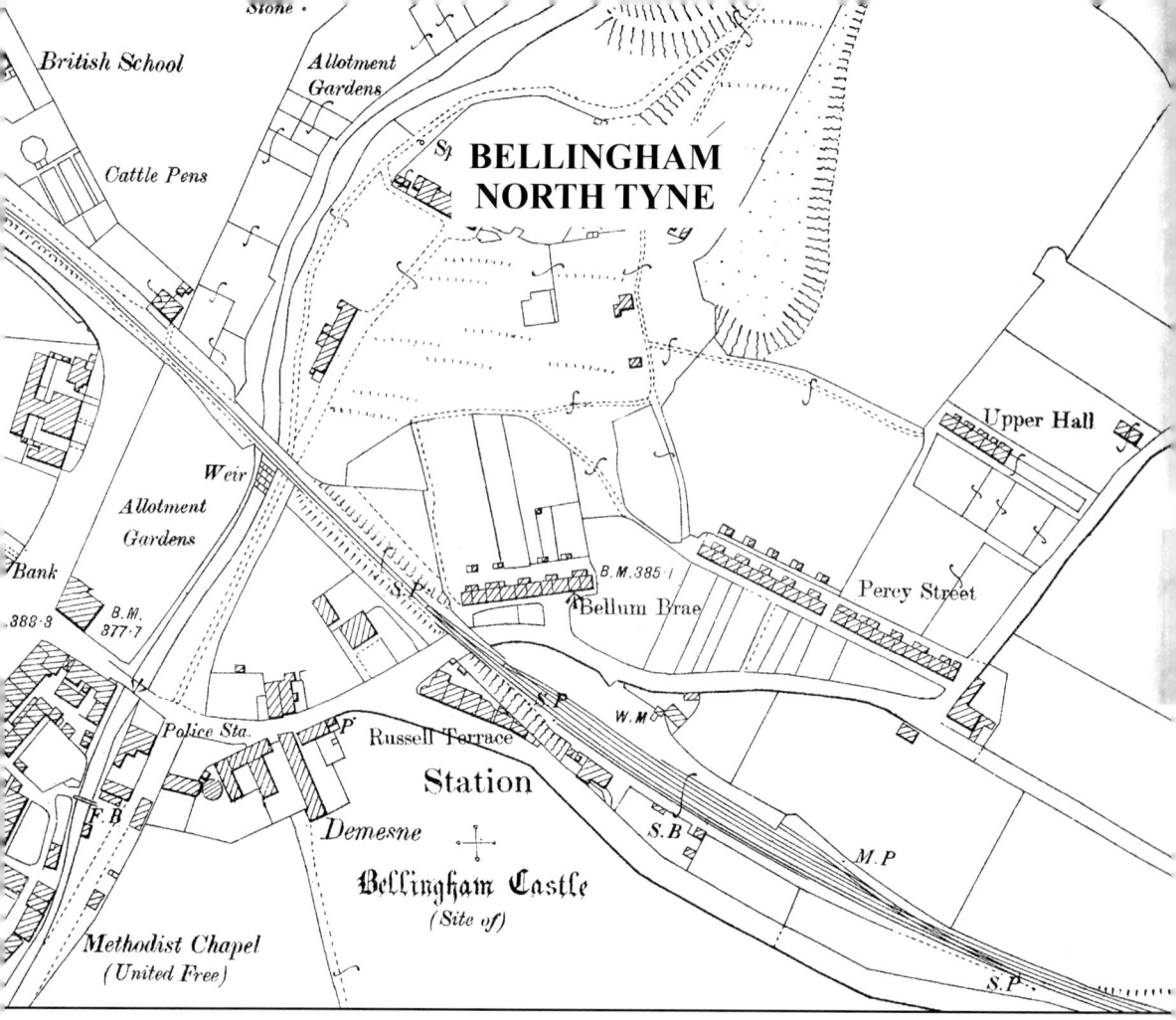

XXVII. Bellingham was the shire town for this part of Northumberland with its agricultural show, cattle market and schools. We end our journey here because this was the terminus of many of the excursion trains on the latter days of the line and because the station is now the Bellingham Heritage Centre. After closure of the Border Counties Railway to goods on 1st September 1956, Bellingham continued to be served by goods trains from the Wansbeck line until 11th November 1963.

BELLINGHAM.

Telegraph station at Hexham, 17 miles.

MARKET DAY.—Saturday.

FAIRS.—May, Saturday before the 12th; September, 1st Wednesday after 15th.

A polling town, situated on the North Tyne, with a population of about 800, principally employed in the mines and quarries, the neighbourhood of which abounds in limestone, coal, and iron.

Extract from Bradshaw's Guide for 1866.
(reprinted by Middleton Press 2011)

More maps and photographs can be found in the *Hexham to Hawick* album on the Border Counties Railway, published by Middleton Press.

119. Bellingham station, signal box and staff with a group of boys pose in this 1910 postcard view. The boys may be waiting for the train for Reedsmouth after school. The station only had one platform though there was a sizeable goods yard and dock. The bridges through Bellingham were built for double track, but there was no attempt to provide the cattle market with its own siding. Animals were unloaded at the dock and driven through the town. (J.Alsop coll.)

120. J36 class (NBR Holmes 'C') no. 5343, on a one coach train in 1946 or 1947, waits in the station. The rear cover continues the Bellingham story. (ARPT)

MP Middleton Press

EVOLVING THE ULTIMATE RAIL ENCYCLOPEDIA

Easebourne Lane, Midhurst, West Sussex.
GU29 9AZ Tel:01730 813169

www.middletonpress.co.uk email:info@middletonpress.co.uk

A-978 0 906520 B- 978 1 873793 C- 978 1 901706 D-978 1 904474
E - 978 1 906008 F - 978 1 908174

All titles listed below were in print at time of publication - please check current availability by looking at our website - *www.middletonpress.co.uk* or by requesting a Brochure which includes our *LATEST* RAILWAY TITLES also our TRAMWAY, TROLLEYBUS, MILITARY and COASTAL series

A

Abergavenny to Merthyr C 91 8
Abertillery & Ebbw Vale Lines D 84 5
Aberystwyth to Carmarthen E 90 1
Allhallows - Branch Line to A 62 8
Alton - Branch Lines to A 11 6
Andover to Southampton A 82 6
Ascot - Branch Lines around A 64 2
Ashburton - Branch Line to B 95 4
Ashford - Steam to Eurostar B 67 1
Ashford to Dover A 48 2
Austrian Narrow Gauge D 04 3
Avonmouth - BL around D 42 5
Aylesbury to Rugby D 91 3

B

Baker Street to Uxbridge D 90 6
Bala to Llandudno E 87 1
Banbury to Birmingham D 27 2
Banbury to Cheltenham E 63 5
Bangor to Holyhead F 01 7
Bangor to Portmadoc E 72 7
Barking to Southend C 80 2
Barmouth to Pwllheli E 53 6
Barry - Branch Lines around D 50 0
Bartlow - Branch Lines to F 27 7
Bath Green Park to Bristol C 36 9
Bath to Evercreech Junction A 60 4
Beamish 40 years on rails E94 9
Bedford to Wellingborough D 31 9
Berwick to Drem F 64 2
Berwick to St. Boswells F 75 8
B'ham to Tamworth & Nuneaton F 63 5
Birkenhead to West Kirby F 61 1
Birmingham to Wolverhampton E253
Bletchley to Cambridge D 94 4
Bletchley to Rugby E 07 9
Bodmin - Branch Lines around B 83 1
Boston to Lincoln F 80 2
Bournemouth to Evercreech Jn A 46 8
Bournemouth to Weymouth A 57 4
Bradshaw's History F18 5
Bradshaw's Rail Times 1850 F 13 0
Bradshaw's Rail Times 1895 F 11 6
Branch Lines series - see town names
Brecon to Neath D 43 2
Brecon to Newport D 16 6
Brecon to Newtown E 06 2
Brighton to Eastbourne A 16 1
Brighton to Worthing A 03 1
Bristol to Taunton D 03 6
Bromley South to Rochester B 23 7
Bromsgrove to Birmingham D 87 6
Bromsgrove to Gloucester D 73 9
Broxbourne to Cambridge F16 1
Brunel - A railtour D 74 6
Bude - Branch Line to B 29 9
Burnham to Evercreech Jn B 68 0

C

Cambridge to Ely D 55 5
Canterbury - BLs around B 58 9
Cardiff to Dowlais (Cae Harris) E 47 5
Cardiff to Pontypridd E 95 6
Cardiff to Swansea E 42 0
Carlisle to Hawick E 85 7
Carmarthen to Fishguard E 66 6
Caterham & Tattenham Corner B251
Central & Southern Spain NG E 91 8
Chard and Yeovil - BLs a C 30 7
Charing Cross to Dartford A 75 8
Charing Cross to Orpington A 96 3
Cheddar - Branch Line to B 90 9
Cheltenham to Andover C 43 7
Cheltenham to Redditch D 81 4
Chester to Birkenhead F 21 5
Chester to Manchester F 51 2
Chester to Rhyl E 93 2
Chester to Warrington F 40 6
Chichester to Portsmouth A 14 7
Clacton and Walton - BLs to F 04 8
Clapham Jn to Beckenham Jn B 36 7
Cleobury Mortimer - BLs a E 18 5
Clevedon & Portishead - BLs to D180
Consett to South Shields E 57 4
Cornwall Narrow Gauge D 56 2
Corris and Vale of Rheidol E 65 9
Craven Arms to Llandeilo E 35 2
Craven Arms to Wellington E 33 8
Crawley to Littlehampton A 34 5
Crewe to Manchester F 57 4
Cromer - Branch Lines around C 26 0
Croydon to East Grinstead B 48 0
Crystal Palace & Catford Loop B 87 1
Cyprus Narrow Gauge E 13 0

D

Darjeeling Revisited F 09 3
Darlington Leamside Newcastle E 28 4
Darlington to Newcastle D 98 2
Dartford to Sittingbourne B 34 3
Denbigh - Branch Lines around F 32 1
Derwent Valley - BL to the D 06 7
Devon Narrow Gauge E 09 3
Didcot to Banbury D 02 9
Didcot to Swindon C 84 0
Didcot to Winchester C 13 0
Dorset & Somerset NG D 76 0
Douglas - Laxey - Ramsey E 75 8
Douglas to Peel C 88 8
Douglas to Port Erin C 55 0
Douglas to Ramsey D 39 5
Dover to Ramsgate A 78 9
Dublin Northwards in 1950s E 31 4
Dunstable - Branch Lines to E 27 7

E

Ealing to Slough C 42 0
Eastbourne to Hastings A 27 7
East Cornwall Mineral Railways D 22 7
East Croydon to Three Bridges A 53 6
Eastern Spain Narrow Gauge E 56 7
East Grinstead - BLs to A 07 9
East London - Branch Lines of C 44 4
East London Line B 80 0
East of Norwich - Branch Lines E 69 7
Effingham Junction - BLs a A 74 1
Ely to Norwich C 90 1
Enfield Town & Palace Gates D 32 6
Epsom to Horsham A 30 7
Eritrean Narrow Gauge E 38 3
Euston to Harrow & Wealdstone C 89 5
Exeter to Barnstaple B 15 2
Exeter to Newton Abbot C 49 9
Exeter to Tavistock B 69 5
Exmouth - Branch Lines to B 00 8

F

Fairford - Branch Line to A 52 9
Falmouth, Helston & St. Ives C 74 1
Fareham to Salisbury A 67 3
Faversham to Dover B 05 3
Felixstowe & Aldeburgh - BL to D 20 3
Fenchurch Street to Barking C 20 8
Festiniog - 50 yrs of enterprise C 83 3
Festiniog 1946-55 E 01 7
Festiniog in the Fifties B 68 8
Festiniog in the Sixties B 91 6
Ffestiniog in Colour 1955-82 F 25 3
Finsbury Park to Alexandra Pal C 02 8
Frome to Bristol B 77 0

G

Galashiels to Edinburgh F 52 9
Gloucester to Bristol D 35 7
Gloucester to Cardiff D 66 1
Gosport - Branch Lines around A 36 9
Greece Narrow Gauge D 72 2

H

Hampshire Narrow Gauge D 36 4
Harrow to Watford D 14 2
Harwich & Hadleigh - BLs to F 02 4
Harz Revisited F 62 8
Hastings to Ashford A 37 6
Hawick to Galashiels F 36 9
Hawkhurst - Branch Line to A 66 6
Hayling - Branch Line to A 12 3
Hay-on-Wye - BL around D 92 0
Haywards Heath to Seaford A 28 4
Hemel Hempstead - BLs to D 88 3
Henley, Windsor & Marlow - BLa C77 2
Hereford to Newport D 54 8
Hertford & Hatfield - BLs a E 58 1
Hertford Loop E 71 0
Hexham to Carlisle D 75 3
Hexham to Hawick F 08 6
Hitchin to Peterborough D 07 4
Holborn Viaduct to Lewisham A 81 9
Horsham - Branch Lines to A 02 4
Huntingdon - Branch Line to A 93 2

I

Ilford to Shenfield C 97 0
Ilfracombe - Branch Line to B 21 3
Industrial Rlys of the South East A 09 3
Ipswich to Saxmundham C 41 3
Isle of Wight Lines - 50 yrs C 12 3
Italy Narrow Gauge F 17 8

K

Kent Narrow Gauge C 45 1
Kidderminster to Shrewsbury E 10 9
Kingsbridge - Branch Line to C 98 7
Kings Cross to Potters Bar E 62 8
King's Lynn to Hunstanton F 58 1
Kingston & Hounslow Loops A 83 3
Kingswear - Branch Line to C 17 8

L

Lambourn - Branch Line to C 70 3
Launceston & Princetown - BLs C 19 2
Lewisham to Dartford A 92 5
Lincoln to Cleethorpes F 56 7
Lines around Wimbledon B 75 6
Liverpool Street to Chingford D 01 2
Liverpool Street to Ilford C 34 5
Llandeilo to Swansea E 46 8
London Bridge to Addiscombe B 20 6
London Bridge to East Croydon A 58 1
Longmoor - Branch Lines to A 41 3
Looe - Branch Line to C 22 2
Loughborough to Nottingham F 68 0
Lowestoft - BLs around E 40 6
Ludlow to Hereford E 14 7
Lydney - Branch Lines around E 26 0
Lyme Regis - Branch Line to A 45 1
Lynton - Branch Line to B 04 6

M

Machynlleth to Barmouth E 54 3
Maesteg and Tondu Lines E 06 2
Majorca & Corsica Narrow Gauge F 41 3
March - Branch Lines around B 09 1
Market Drayton - BLs around F 67 3
Marylebone to Rickmansworth D 49 4
Melton Constable to Yarmouth Bch E031
Midhurst - Branch Lines of E 78 9
Midhurst - Branch Lines to F 00 0
Minehead - Branch Line to A 80 2
Mitcham Junction Lines B 01 5
Monmouth - Branch Lines to E 20 8
Monmouthshire Eastern Valleys D 71 5
Moretonhampstead - BL to C 27 7
Moreton-in-Marsh to Worcester D 26 5
Mountain Ash to Neath D 80 7

N

Newark to Doncaster F 78 9
Newbury to Westbury C 66 6
Newcastle to Hexham D 69 2
Newport (IOW) - Branch Lines to A 26 0
Newquay - Branch Lines to C 71 0
Newton Abbot to Plymouth C 60 4
Newtown to Aberystwyth E 41 3
North East German NG D 44 9
Northern Alpine Narrow Gauge F 37 6
Northern France Narrow Gauge C 75 8
Northern Spain Narrow Gauge E 83 3
North London Line B 94 7
North of Birmingham F 55 0
North Woolwich - BLs around C 65 9
Nottingham to Boston F 70 3
Nottingham to Lincoln F 43 7

O

Ongar - Branch Line to E 05 5
Orpington to Tonbridge B 03 9
Oswestry - Branch Lines around E 60 4
Oswestry to Whitchurch E 81 9
Oxford to Bletchley D 57 9
Oxford to Moreton-in-Marsh D 15 9

P

Paddington to Ealing C 37 6
Paddington to Princes Risborough C819
Padstow - Branch Line to B 54 1
Pembroke and Cardigan - BLs to F 29 1
Peterborough to Kings Lynn E 32 1
Peterborough to Newark F 72 7
Plymouth - BLs around B 98 5
Plymouth to St. Austell C 63 5
Pontypool to Mountain Ash D 65 4
Pontypridd to Merthyr F 14 7
Pontypridd to Port Talbot E 86 4
Porthmadog 1954-94 - BLa B 31 2
Portmadoc 1923-46 - BLa B 13 8
Portsmouth to Southampton A 31 4
Portugal Narrow Gauge E 67 3
Potters Bar to Cambridge D 70 8
Princes Risborough - BL to D 05 0
Princes Risborough to Banbury C 85 7

R

Railways to Victory C 16 1
Reading to Basingstoke B 27 5
Reading to Didcot C 79 6
Reading to Guildford A 47 5
Redhill to Ashford A 73 4
Return to Blaenau 1970-82 C 64 2
Rhyl to Bangor F 15 4
Rhymney & New Tredegar Lines E 48 2
Rickmansworth to Aylesbury D 61 6
Romania & Bulgaria NG E 23 9
Romneyrail C 32 1
Ross-on-Wye - BLs around E 30 7
Ruabon to Barmouth E 84 0
Rugby to Birmingham E 37 6
Rugby to Loughborough F 12 3
Rugby to Stafford F 07 9
Ryde to Ventnor A 19 2

S

Salisbury to Westbury B 39 8
Sardinia and Sicily Narrow Gauge F 50 5
Saxmundham to Yarmouth C 69 7
Saxony & Baltic Germany Revisited F 71 0
Saxony Narrow Gauge D 47 0
Seaton & Sidmouth - BLs to A 95 6
Selsey - Branch Line to A 04 8
Sheerness - Branch Line to B 16 2
Shenfield to Ipswich E 96 3
Shrewsbury - Branch Line to A 86 4
Shrewsbury to Chester E 70 3
Shrewsbury to Crewe F 48 2
Shrewsbury to Ludlow E 21 5
Shrewsbury to Newtown E 29 1
Sierra Leone Narrow Gauge D 28 9
Sirhowy Valley Line E 12 3
Sittingbourne to Ramsgate A 90 1
Slough to Newbury C 56 7
South African Two-foot gauge E 51 2
Southampton to Bournemouth A 42 0
Southend & Southminster BLs E 76 5
Southern Alpine Narrow Gauge F 22 2
Southern France Narrow Gauge C 47 5
South London Line B 46 6
South Lynn to Norwich City F 03 1
Southwold - Branch Line to A 15 4
Spalding - Branch Lines around E 52 9
Spalding to Grimsby F 65 9 6
Stafford to Chester F 34 5
Stafford to Wellington F 59 8
St Albans to Bedford D 08 1
St. Austell to Penzance C 67 3
St. Boswell to Berwick F 44 4
Steaming Through Isle of Wight A
Steaming Through West Hants A
Stourbridge to Wolverhampton E
St. Pancras to Barking D 68 5
St. Pancras to Folkestone E 88 8
St. Pancras to St. Albans C 78 9
Stratford to Cheshunt F 53 6
Stratford-u-Avon to Birmingham D
Stratford-u-Avon to Cheltenham C
Sudbury - Branch Lines to F 19 2
Surrey Narrow Gauge C 87 1
Sussex Narrow Gauge C 68 0
Swanley to Ashford B 45 9
Swansea - Branch Lines around F
Swansea to Carmarthen E 59 8
Swindon to Bristol C 96 3
Swindon to Gloucester D 46 3
Swindon to Newport D 30 2
Swiss Narrow Gauge C 94 9

T

Talyllyn 60 E 98 7
Tamworth to Derby F 76 5
Taunton to Barnstaple B 60 2
Taunton to Exeter C 82 6
Taunton to Minehead F 39 0
Tavistock to Plymouth B 88 6
Tenterden - Branch Line to A 21 5
Three Bridges to Brighton A 35 2
Tilbury Loop C 86 4
Tiverton - BLs around C 62 8
Tivetshall to Beccles D 41 8
Tonbridge to Hastings A 44 4
Torrington - Branch Lines to B 37
Towcester - BLs around E 39 0
Tunbridge Wells BLs A 32 1

U

Upwell - Branch Line to B 64 0

V

Victoria to Bromley South A 98 7
Victoria to East Croydon A 40 6
Vivarais Revisited E 08 6

W

Walsall Routes F 45 1
Wantage - Branch Line to D 25 8
Wareham to Swanage 50 yrs D09
Waterloo to Windsor A 54 3
Waterloo to Woking A 38 3
Watford to Leighton Buzzard D 45
Wellingborough to Leicester F 73
Welshpool to Llanfair E 49 9
Wenford Bridge to Fowey C 09 3
Westbury to Bath B 55 8
Westbury to Taunton C 76 5
West Cornwall Mineral Rlys D 48
West Croydon to Epsom B 08 4
West German Narrow Gauge D 93
West London - BLs of C 50 5
West London Line B 84 8
West Wiltshire - BLs of D 12 8
Weymouth - BLs A 65 9
Willesden Jn to Richmond B 71 8
Wimbledon to Beckenham C 58 1
Wimbledon to Epsom B 62 6
Wimborne - BLs around A 97 0
Wisbech - BLs around C 01 7
Witham & Kelvedon - BLs a E 82 6
Woking to Alton A 59 8
Woking to Portsmouth A 25 3
Woking to Southampton A 55 0
Wolverhampton to Shrewsbury E4
Wolverhampton to Stafford F 79 6
Worcester to Birmingham D 97 5
Worcester to Hereford D 38 8
Worthing to Chichester A 06 2
Wrexham to New Brighton F 47 5
Wroxham - BLs around F 31 4

Y

Yeovil - 50 yrs change C 38 3
Yeovil to Dorchester A 76 5
Yeovil to Exeter A 91 8
York to Scarborough F 23 9